# EMPOWERING DYSLEXIA

Proven Tools & Strategies For
Parents & Teachers To **Foster Reading**
& **Inspire Dyslexic Brilliance** In Children

A. Marie

# Contents

# References

# Free Gift!

T hank you for taking the time to read this book and for your dedication in supporting children with dyslexia.

It's readers like you who make a true difference, and I couldn't be more grateful to have you here. To add even more value to your journey, I've created an exclusive bonus bundle just for you!

**What's inside:**

**1. Simple, Ready-to-Use Activities:** You'll find practical tools you can start using right away to bring more ease and creativity into learning. These resources are here to save you time and make every small win feel meaningful.

**2. Confidence Boosts for Kids:** With tips focused on building self-esteem, this bundle helps kids feel strong, proud, and capable. It's all about uplifting their confidence and celebrating who they are.

**3. Everyday Tips for Real-Life Impact:** Each resource is designed to fit naturally into daily routines, making it easier to support and encourage learning in simple, enjoyable ways.

To receive **this for free**, follow these simple steps:

Visit https://mariepublications.com/freeguide

**OR**

Simply scan the QR code below:

It's quick and easy! By taking this step, you'll gain access to this valuable guide at no cost. Enjoy!

# Introduction

I had a very basic understanding of dyslexia and how it affects people. Like many others, I mistakenly believed it affected only how a person saw letters, numbers, and words. It was as simple as seeing words backwards as if it were a vision problem that made reading difficult. I also assumed dyslexia applied only to the English language. Boy, was I wrong about everything!

**Let me tell you some of Clayton's story.**

I met Clayton while affiliated with a dyslexia program in a prominent Texas city. He was an intelligent, witty, happy little kid... who didn't like school.

He didn't long to be at home or miss Mom and Dad. He was quite sociable and is still in touch with some of those early friends.

He didn't dislike his teacher either. Though she insisted he do the assignments he truly couldn't grasp, he enjoyed being in her class.

But then first grade rolled around.

In first grade, Clayton continued to be his cheerful, upbeat self... except when it came to school. He was forced to sit still at his desk and struggled with reading, writing, and math, his frustration often leading him to stare out the window or chew on his pencils.

He understood the concepts his teacher taught and found some of them to be quite interesting.

He wanted to do the work and had a great desire to learn.

He wasn't "retarded" either, as his teacher told his parents he was.

As I said, Clayton was intelligent! (He still is, of course.) His teacher couldn't see that Clayton couldn't see things the way the majority of the population does. His brain is wired a bit differently—very uniquely, actually—almost like a super-hero's!

Clayton has the extraordinary ability to turn letters upside down and make them dance and shape-shift! He pulls forms out from a flat surface into three dimensions. He can also solve math problems that don't appear on the page, where the numbers shift to the right or move to the top of the equation, allowing him to create a solution different from what was initially presented.

As you might imagine, these superpowers can transform a standard classroom into a torture chamber.

When learning the printed alphabet, Clayton noticed that the letter "B" looked different every time he saw it. While she was still figuring out how to help her son learn, Clayton's mom would get flustered when he'd correctly identify a letter—let's stick with "B"—on a flashcard but have no clue what that same "B" was when she showed it to him again. He didn't know it because, to him, it didn't look like "B" anymore. His eyes saw it dance and shape-shift into an "F"? A "Z"? A creature from *Star Wars*?

Now, imagine trying to read a word, sentence, paragraph, or even a book full of letters that think they're at a masquerade ball. Deciphering written language can be quite difficult, can't it?

**Also, consider Christian's story.**

I met nine-year-old Christian at the school he attended in a slum in Caracas, Venezuela. He was often disruptive in class, which caused problems for the teacher and other students.

Christian could spell his name but not his mother's or sister's. When I dictated the letters to him, he looked at me with embarrassment and shame.

It seemed strange—how could he spell his own name but not the names of the two most influential people in his life? The answer was simple: Christian had memorized the sequence of letters in his name, which allowed him to spell it. However, he still struggled with identifying the sounds of each letter.

For example, if I asked him to spell "mom," he couldn't break down the sounds of "m" or "o." He recognized "Christian" as a single unit, like a picture, rather than a series of individual sounds. It was like recognizing the shape of a stop sign but not being able to read the word "STOP" on it.

Despite this, it was clear that he was an intelligent kid, but around him, Christian's classmates taunted, "Christian doesn't know how to read or write. He's stupid!" He didn't lack intelligence, but even I initially thought he might be illiterate, given his vulnerable background. But I was wrong—he wasn't illiterate. He had dyslexia.

That evening, I phoned my mom, who's a specialist in the area of special education. She recognized the symptoms of severe dyslexia before I could even give her all the details. Knowing I'd only be with this program for three months, I asked her how to help Christian in such a short time. She advised me to begin by building his self-esteem. Her exact words were, "You need to tell him he is not stupid, and he can make it in life regardless of his circumstances. Teach him what dyslexia is, how it affects him, and how to stand up for himself."

I began working with Christian as my mother suggested, and I also educated his teachers and the other professionals I was working with because none of them had experience or training with dyslexia either.

## Understanding Dyslexia

As you can see from Clayton's and Christian's stories, dyslexia has nothing to do with a person's intellect, vision, hearing or social class. Research has shown that the brain's physical structure, chemical composition, and processing functionality differ in individuals with dyslexia compared to those who don't have it. Only about 7% of people worldwide are diagnosed with dyslexia, but many more go undiagnosed because their symptoms aren't severe enough to seek treatment (Cleveland Clinic, n.d.-c). Altogether, how 20% of the population views information on a page, processes and categorizes it, and applies it in their lives looks strange to the other 80% (*Dyslexia FAQ*, n.d.). Because it's not what most people know to be "normal," it is very often misunderstood, even within medical and counselling communities.

This alternate way of processing means people with dyslexia have unique learning styles and require academic instruction that caters to how they receive information. Clayton was fortunate to grow up in an urban area in the United States, have supportive parents, and be able to seek out and acquire the help he needed. That, sadly, is not the case for many others, including Christian. Plenty of cities and towns in the United States and around the globe lack knowledge, training, and resources on dyslexia and how to manage it.

That's why I've written this book. Even with a degree in psychology and having a parent in the special needs field, I was very unprepared to help Christian, and so were the people who should have been his support network. My goal with this book is to enable parents, educators, and people with dyslexia themselves to recognize the potential of dyslexic learners and empower them to excel in academic, creative, and personal realms.

EMPOWERING DYSLEXIA: PROVEN TOOLS & STRATEGIES FOR PARENTS & TEACHERS TO FOSTER READING & INSPIRE DYSLEXIC BRILLIANCE IN CHILDREN presents the groundbreaking MORE framework—a revolutionary approach to understanding and cultivating dyslexic brilliance. Its mission is to empower and inspire confidence in children with dyslexia by reframing the condition not as a *disability* but as a unique *ability*. Dyslexia doesn't make anyone less; it makes them more—MORE capable, MORE skilled, MORE creative, and MORE talented than they or society often recognize.

The MORE framework highlights four main strengths of dyslexic minds:

- **M**ultifaceted ingenuity: People with dyslexia are often very clever and creative. We'll explore the diverse ways in which they think and perceive the world.

- **O**ut-of-the-box thinking: People with dyslexia tend to think outside the box by generating innovative solutions and inventive ideas. We'll discuss actionable strategies for leveraging these strengths.

- **R**easoning: People with dyslexia approach issues with unique logical, spatial, narrative, and dynamic reasoning. We'll examine ways to empower dyslexic children to utilize these aptitudes and excel academically and beyond.

- **E**xpression: People with dyslexia can be very imaginative, express themselves creatively, and empathize with others. We'll look at ways to nurture these qualities in your child.

What if the key to unlocking the world's greatest potential lies within the MORE unique minds of these individuals? As we progress through this book, we'll gain an understanding of this condition, see what the world looks like through the eyes of people with dyslexia, and examine the strengths they possess. Along the way, we'll check back in with Clayton and Christian and see how we can apply their real-life experiences to help kids in any situation get the support they need. Together, we can make the world a better place for learners with dyslexia and offer them a future of endless possibilities.

# Part 1: The Dimensions of Dyslexia

## Chapter 1

# What the World Is Like With Dyslexia

*Dyslexia is not a pigeonhole to say you can't do anything. It is an opportunity and a possibility to learn differently. You have magical brains, they just process differently. Don't feel like you should be held back by it.*

—Her Royal Highness Princess Beatrice

D yslexia is considered to be a learning challenge because it disrupts how the brain receives and interprets written information. A person can be mildly affected, meaning they have some struggles but are able to work around them; moderately affected, meaning their afflictions are challenging enough to require assistance and intervention; or severely affected, meaning their symptoms are so pronounced that even with accommodations and treatments, they still have extreme hardships. Reading difficulty is the most common symptom and one of the main identifiers, but the disorder affects other aspects of learning, decision-making, and behaviour.

## The Neurological Landscape

Though classified as a disorder, dyslexia is really the result of the brain finding a different way to process language and certain other information than what is considered the norm. When viewed this way, it's actually a superpower, but sadly, people rarely recognize children with dyslexia as heroes.

I worked with seven-year-old Michael, another child who struggled in the classroom at an urban inner-city school in Canada. He experienced a combination of Clayton's and Christian's symptoms. When he tried to write his name, it always appeared backwards on the paper as if he'd been looking at it in the mirror. Michael's teacher seated him at the back of the classroom so he wouldn't distract or slow down other students, and he was often the subject of mockery.

After observing possible dyslexic tendencies in Michael's behaviour, I spoke with his teacher about potential accommodations that would help him in the classroom.

With her patient instruction, Michael has gained self-understanding and learned tools to help his dyslexia work *for* him rather than *against* him.

The brain's neurological functions work differently in dyslexic minds than in people without this learning difference.

These physiological aspects do not hinder or negatively impact intelligence at all, but they do alter how information is received and interpreted.

In the pages ahead, we'll examine this more closely, see what signs and symptoms may reveal dyslexic tendencies, and discuss the importance of early intervention. Along the way, we'll also debunk some common myths about dyslexia.

# The Brain's Pathways: Reading Through a Dyslexic Lens

Researchers have identified two cognitive processes involved in reading: grapheme-phoneme mapping and visual word recognition. In the first process, graphemes, which are letter combinations, are mapped onto phonemes, which are the corresponding sounds of those letters or letter combinations.

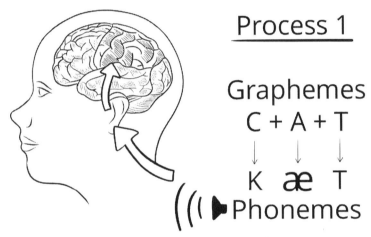

*For instance, take the word "cat." In the first process, each letter (or grapheme) in "cat"—'c', 'a', and 't'—is matched to its corresponding sound (or phoneme): /k/, /æ/, and /t/. This way, the letters are mapped to the sounds they represent, helping to form the spoken word.*

From there, the brain visually interprets the words and connects them to the meaning we already know in our minds. For example, when you see the word "cat," your brain not only processes the sounds of each letter but also instantly links the word to the image of a small, furry animal you recognize as a cat. Once that's understood, certain brain regions enable you to verbally say "cat." Recent studies have shown that this reading system occurs in the brain's left hemisphere and involves the occipitotemporal, temporoparietal, and inferior frontal cortices. These key regions, physiologically altered in people with dyslexia, enable us to form speech sounds. (*Dyslexia and the Brain*, n.d.).

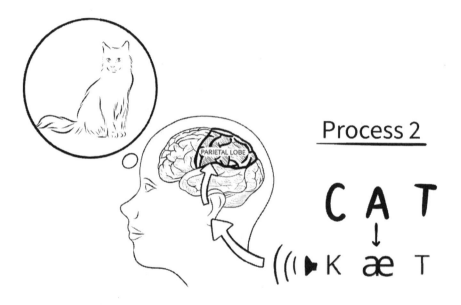

In psychology, the dominant theory is that the brain operates laterally rather than holistically. This means it's compartmentalized into two main hemispheres and further delineated by specific areas or lobes specializing in distinct tasks instead of working as one whole unit. For example, certain regions interpret, process, and form language, while others direct physical movements or manage memories.

In non-dyslexic individuals, several regions of the brain have left-right asymmetry, meaning the left and right sides of the brain are structurally unique and perform different functions. However, examination of brain autopsies from adults who had dyslexia and MRI scans of individuals living with the condition have revealed missing asymmetries in key brain regions. These differences are found in areas responsible for language and reading, like the temporal lobe, where expected size variations are absent, specifically the occipitotemporal region, which handles word recognition, and the temporoparietal region, which processes word sounds. Other studies indicate people with less brain asymmetry may be prone to "less effective thought processes" (Gamma, 2023). While this information is still being studied, it demonstrates a physical difference in the brains of those with dyslexia and those without.

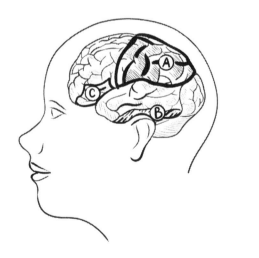

# Process 3

(A) Temporoparietal

(B) Occipitotemporal

(C) Inferior Frontal Cortices

Also, functional magnetic resonance imaging (fMRI) has gained popularity in studying people with and without dyslexia. Instead of viewing the brain at rest, fMRI measures the brain's neural activation while it is engaged in activity. These results have repeatedly shown that people with dyslexia have underactive brain areas related to word and language processing. To compensate for this, other brain areas, like those for problem-solving and creativity, become more active. This overcompensation often helps the child excel in those areas, but it can also mask dyslexia, making it harder to diagnose.

Take, for example, Percy, age 14, who was described in the *British Medical Journal* as a student who "has always been a bright and intelligent boy, quick at games, and in no way inferior to others of his age. His great difficulty has been—and is now—his inability to read" (Hudson et al., n.d.). Though weak in reading, he excelled in other areas, such as problem-solving and creativity.

Clayton's mom, Vicki, found this to be true of herself. Growing up, she was a star athlete, popular, and very social. She earned a full scholarship to a prominent university as a softball pitcher, but academics—particularly English and math—stumped her, and she always felt like there was something weird about herself. Vicki never knew she had dyslexia until her son was diagnosed!

These stories show how dyslexia can be easily overlooked when children excel in other areas, making diagnosis more challenging.

# Dysgraphia, Dyscalculia, and Dyslexia

The Cleveland Clinic says dyslexia is considered a "specific learning disorder" that has three subtypes: dysgraphia (writing), dyscalculia (mathematics), and dyslexia (reading). A person can display one or any combination of the three (n.d.-c).

## *Dysgraphia*

The Cleveland Clinic defines dysgraphia as "a neurological condition and learning difference in which someone has difficulty with writing for their age level" (n.d.-b). They may have problems with the physical act of writing or transforming their thoughts into written words. It has no cure but is manageable.

Writing asks a lot of the brain. It requires conceptualization, organization, letter memory and coding, language processing, and fine motor skills. Dysgraphia usually appears in children when they are learning to write, but it can also develop as a result of head trauma or brain injury.

Here are some of the signs of dysgraphia:

- Lack of fine motor mastery

- Difficulty using a pen or pencil

- Slow writing

- Writing letters backward

- Illegible letters and numbers

- Irregular letter size

- Inability to recall letter shapes

- Spelling difficulty

- Confusion with upper and lower case letters

- Inconsistent spacing between letters and words

- Inability to write in a straight line

- Improper grammar usage

- Writing words in the wrong order in sentences

- Leaving words out of sentences

Though separate from dyslexia, it is often a comorbid condition accompanying dyslexia, dyscalculia, attention deficit disorder (ADD), attention deficit hyperactivity disorder (ADHD), or autism spectrum disorder (ASD). It is more common in males than females and has genetic links.

## Dyscalculia

Like dysgraphia, dyscalculia can develop independently or in combination with dyslexia, dysgraphia, ADHD, ASD, or other conditions. The Cleveland Clinic defines dyscalculia as "a learning disorder that affects a person's ability to understand number-based information and math" (n.d.-a). It differs from struggling to recall addition facts or times tables; people with dyscalculia do not *process* math-related concepts in the same manner as those without it. Because of this processing irregularity, having to perform even basic math operations can ignite anxiety, panic, and depression and lead to embarrassment, low self-esteem, and a lack of self-confidence.

Solving math problems requires the brain to process equations visually, call on the memory to recognize numbers (and sometimes letters) as well as various symbols and how to solve the problem, utilize language processing to interpret what the symbols mean, comprehend quantities and relate them to the correct numerals, and then, of course, calculate the solution. People with dyscalculia may struggle with any or all parts of the process.

Here are some common signs of dyscalculia:

- Difficulty counting forward or backward

- Inability to identify the correct numeral to represent an amount

- Unable to recognize numbers and symbols

- Trouble with ordering numbers

- Not understanding number lines

- Confusion when learning about money

- Counting on fingers at an age when they should be well past that

- Inability to solve equations in their head

- Trouble memorizing and reciting math facts

- Difficulty solving word problems

Clayton has a combination of dyslexia and dyscalculia. Not only does dyslexia transform the shapes of numbers, letters, and symbols, but dyscalculia also rearranges their order within the problems and causes his brain to solve an entirely different equation.

IF HE IS GIVEN **437-213=?,**
HE MIGHT INTERPRET IT AS **31Z-732=?**

In addition to these characteristics, fear, anxiety, anger, aggression, and physical manifestations of those emotions like headache, stomachache, nausea, vomiting, and sweating can compound the child's frustration.

People with dyscalculia are also at higher risk of developing bipolar disorder, oppositional defiant disorder, and other mental health conditions. While it is suspected to be genetic, it may also relate to differences in how the parts of the brain that manage mathematical functions are structured compared to those without dyscalculia.

## *Dyslexia*

According to the Cleveland Clinic, dyslexia is "a learning disability that disrupts how your brain processes written language" (n.d.-c). Though it is treatable, it is not curable. However, as you'll see later on, when we read more of Clayton's story, it can be a smooth process to success.

Dyslexia primarily affects reading and language-related tasks. As mentioned above, it disrupts language interpretation processes, specifically of written letters, words, and numbers.

Children first learn language by hearing others speak to them. They gradually learn that the sounds they hear are related to specific shapes or characters, such as letters and numbers. The brains of children with dyslexia don't properly break down the sounds they hear and the symbols they see. This can result in slow reading, difficulty with spelling and writing, an inability to form sentences that communicate complex thoughts, and problems with word storage in the memory.

As a kid, Clayton, taking after his dad, grandpa, and great-grandpa, was an entertaining storyteller. He could weave words masterfully to compete with *Beowulf* and keep the listener spellbound. He had no trouble putting words together to create simple or complex sentences or piecing sentences together to tell a tall tale, but he couldn't properly put them down on paper. Even through college, when Clayton wrote, everything ran together without punctuation, capitalization, or paragraph breaks. His thoughts must flow until he fully expresses them because the words are not stored long-term in his memory. He also struggles with short-term memory issues regarding ordinary, everyday life.

## Contributing Factors

Experts don't know the exact cause of dyslexia, but these may be contributing factors:

- **Genetics:** When one parent has dyslexia, there's a 30–50% chance their child may inherit it (Cleveland Clinic, n.d.-c).

- **Toxic exposure:** If the child's mother was exposed to harmful chemicals like water pollution, air pollution, heavy metals, flame retardants, and nicotine while pregnant, the fetus could have been affected.

- **Different brain structures:** Certain brain traits differ between individuals with and without dyslexia, potentially influencing its occurrence.

## Signs of Dyslexia

Dyslexia is primarily seen as a reading disorder, and most individuals affected by it face challenges in this area. However, it can also manifest in other difficulties like spelling, writing, speaking, sounding out words, and comprehending written words. It can also extend beyond these academic skills to problem-solving, social interactions, and internalizing general information.

Here are some ways to recognize dyslexia at various ages (The Understood Team, n.d.-b):

- **Preschool**

  - Difficulty following directions

  - Telling stories that are not in a logical order

  - Having trouble remembering sequences, like the letters of the alphabet

  - Mispronouncing familiar words, like "beary tear" instead of "teddy bear."

- **Kindergarten through 2nd grade**

  - Difficulty learning letter names and sounds

  - Difficulty remembering and applying spelling rules

  - Confusing letters that look similar, like d/b and p/q

  - Having trouble pronouncing familiar words, like "cat," if there's not an accompanying picture

  - Having trouble separating individual sounds and blending sounds

- **3rd through 5th grade**

  - Avoiding reading or getting upset and frustrated while reading

  - Reversing letters

- Spelling words incorrectly

- Skipping small words when reading aloud

- Difficulty sounding out new words

- **6th grade through adulthood**

  - Leaving out words and reading very slowly when reading aloud

  - Answering comprehension questions more easily when the text is read aloud to them

  - Difficulty remembering common abbreviations

  - Difficulty understanding puns and word jokes

  - Taking an extraordinarily long time to read

  - Difficulty thinking of synonyms

No medications treat dyslexia. Educational interventions are most effective, like learning new ways to read, working with a tutor, and partnering with your child's school to ensure they get the assistance they need.

## *How Is Dyslexia Diagnosed?*

Diagnosing a child with dyslexia can be challenging because they may not present enough symptoms early on and because some characteristics can also indicate other issues like vision or hearing deficits.

If you are concerned about your child, the first step you should take is to talk to their teacher. Kids sometimes perform differently for their parents than they do at school, and the teacher would be able to confirm or deny suspicions you have about reading, writing, or learning difficulties.

It would be best to have your child evaluated by their pediatrician or general practitioner to rule out underlying health problems and discuss the possibility of dyslexia with them. They can refer you to an educational psychologist or qualified specialist for testing and treatment. However, an assessment may need to be requested by your child's teacher or the school's special needs coordinator.

Dyslexia assessments look at the following criteria:

- Speaking skills

- Word recognition

- Sounding out unfamiliar words

- Reading fluency

- Reading comprehension

- Spelling and vocabulary

After making a diagnosis, your child's school can work with you to make necessary accommodations or develop an individualized education program (IEP). They may also recommend resources and therapy centers where your child can receive additional assistance.

In general, educational interventions for all three subtypes are categorized as follows:

- **Accommodation:** Your child can access the school's regular curriculum and is provided additional resources, but the educational content does not require customization.

- **Modification:** The school provides extra resources and services to your child and modifies classroom aspects to work with your child's abilities, like allowing your child to answer tests orally instead of writing out answers.

- **Remediation:** Specific interventions may include extra time for reading assignments, using audiobooks for complex texts, and breaking down instructions into smaller, manageable steps. In the classroom, teachers might use visual aids, reading guides, and hands-on activities to support the child's learning.

Always advocate for your child! After attending workshops for parents of children with dyslexia, Vicki and Tom, Clayton's parents, decided to fund training for every teacher and administrator at Clayton's school, ensuring they understood dyslexia and had the tools to support students with different learning needs. Granted, not everyone is in a position to provide that level of training to all of their child's teachers, but it is important to work alongside your child's school system to make sure your child has access to the resources they need and can get the education they deserve.

## Beyond Book Learning

Let's continue Vicki's story. Though she always felt some-thing was different about her, she never thought she had dyslexia. The term "dyslexia" originated in 1883, but only in recent decades has it become understood and given proper attention. When Vicki was a kid, it was unheard of, and her school struggles weren't severe enough for her, her parents, or her teachers to consider a learning disability. It never crossed their minds until Vicki learned that "A child with a parent who has dyslexia has a 30% to 50% chance of inherit-ing it." She and her husband, Tom, then attended workshops to understand better what living with this learning difference looked, sounded, and felt like for a child (Cleveland Clinic, n.d.-c).

Vicki, Tom, and a group of other parents were put through three different experiences:

- For the first one, they were to view the reflection of an object in a mirror and then draw the reflected image on paper without looking back at the mirror. Tom did it without any trouble, but Vicki—even though she had artistic ability—could not recreate the image.

- The second task took them into a room filled with the sound of 100 call center representatives, all talking at once and taking customer orders. Their "job" was to listen to the "customer" on their phone and take down all the details. Again, Tom did just fine, but Vicki struggled to isolate her customer's voice from the overwhelming chatter. She even found herself physically leaning into the speaker to hear better.

- The final activity was to speed-read a passage and summarize it. Once more, Tom completed it easily, but Vicki couldn't do it. She tried to skim the story but did not pick up on any keywords or phrases and missed the entire point of the passage.

In a moment of realization, Vicki sat back and said, "Tom, I'm dyslexic!"

Because Vicki didn't struggle with backward, dancing, or mis-shapen letters, she never suspected that dyslexia was the strangeness she always felt about herself. As you can see, this learning difference goes far beyond just how a person sees letters on a page—reflections don't make sense, dominant sounds get lost in background noise, and instead of keywords, letters endlessly chase each other.

## Changing the Narrative

The dyslexic brain is formed differently and, therefore, processes information in atypical ways—but those are not *bad*. Let me say that again: **Different does not equal bad.**

While Clayton struggled to read words on a page, he understood spoken and visual information better than his peers, who could read the words themselves. When someone read a book aloud or narrated it in audio format, Clayton could picture the story unfolding in his mind like a movie. This dyslexia super-skill began to benefit Clayton in real-life situations. He became an excellent listener and developed great social skills as a result. As an adult now, he credits this as a silver lining to the dark cloud dyslexia can often be.

Remember when I said Clayton creates solutions to math problems that don't exist? Do you know what that has helped him do? Increase the profitability of the company he works for by 25%. Remember when I said Clayton was an enchanting storyteller? Do you know what this ability to keep listeners engaged has helped him do? Increase the productivity of the department he works in by 400%! Under his management, employees learned to care about their work, themselves, and each other because Clayton has superhero compassion that compensates for his struggles in reading and writing. He listened, he cared, and he gave them validation in return. He made them feel valued and wanted. Ironically, those were things his school peers and some educators did not offer him in his youth.

Clayton's story proves that a brain wired differently can unlock unique strengths. While dyslexia made reading and writing a challenge, it sharpened his listening skills, creativity, and empathy—qualities that now fuel his success in both his career and personal life. His story reminds us that being "different" isn't a setback but a unique strength waiting to be unlocked.

# Truth or Myth? Time to Debunk Dyslexia

- **Myth**: Dyslexia is just about seeing letters and numbers backward.

  - **Debunked**: Reversed letters and numbers are just one possible symptom. Sometimes, they wiggle, flip, twist, turn upside down, switch places, change into other symbols, or disappear altogether.

- **Myth**: Those with dyslexia see everything backwards.

  - **Debunked**: Dyslexia is not a vision disorder, so it doesn't cause people to perceive their surroundings in an unusual way. It applies only to the written language-processing portions of the brain.

- **Myth**: Kids with dyslexia can't read because they don't even try to learn how.

  - **Debunked**: Reading difficulties aren't intentional. As mentioned earlier, letters may appear to shift, but the real difference lies in how the brain is wired. In kids with dyslexia, the brain processes information differently than what is considered normal, which makes learning how to read in a traditional way challenging.

- **Myth**: Once they learn to read, their dyslexia will go away.

  - **Debunked**: Dyslexia is a neurological condition, not a skill to perfect or eliminate.

- **Myth**: To cure it, you just need to read more.

  - **Debunked**: Dyslexia is an affliction in the way the brain functions. In this case, practice won't make perfect.

- **Myth**: You don't show signs of dyslexia until elementary school.

  - **Debunked**: When children typically start recognizing letters, numbers, shapes, and colours, they might see them differently—letters may appear jumbled or reversed, and numbers or shapes might be harder to distinguish. They may also mix up the order of words when speaking, saying "burple pear" instead of "purple bear."

- **Myth**: Dyslexia only occurs with English letters and numbers.

  - **Debunked**: Dyslexia is a problem with processing written language—any language—and has to do with the brain's interpretation of the images it sees.

- **Myth**: Smart people don't get dyslexia.

  - **Debunked**: Dyslexia has nothing to do with a person's level of intelligence.

- **Myth**: You can outgrow dyslexia.

  - **Debunked**: The brain's structure differs in individuals with dyslexia, and that will not change no matter how old they get.

- **Myth**: People with dyslexia are unable to read, and they will never have the ability to.

  - **Debunked**: People with dyslexia *can* read, though they have great difficulty and may read very slowly. Depending on their severity level and how dyslexia affects them, it can be more challenging for some individuals than others.

- **Myth**: Dyslexia is caused by eye problems; they need glasses or surgery.

  - **Debunked**: Dyslexia has nothing to do with how well a person's eyes work. They could have perfect vision and still experience this learning difference.

- **Myth**: Teachers and reading specialists are highly trained to recognize and treat dyslexia.

  - **Debunked**: Most educators have little to no knowledge about dyslexia, how to recognize it, or how to teach this unique learning difference.

As you gain a clearer perspective and come to understand all the implications of dyslexia, you'll develop a new appreciation for those who are affected by it. You will be able to help them see their diagnosis not as a *dis*ability but as a *different ability*. Again, *different does not equal bad.* As we'll see in the chapters ahead, *different equals awesome!*

\*\*\*

# Summary

In this chapter, we've uncovered how the brain processes language and written information in unique ways for those with dyslexia, shedding light on the challenges they face and the resilience they show in overcoming them. We also explored the neurological workings of the brain, focusing on the cognitive processes involved in reading and the brain differences observed in individuals with dyslexia. We followed that by mentioning the potential co-occurring conditions, dysgraphia and dyscalculia, and highlighted the crucial role of early intervention.

In the next chapter, we'll dive into a powerful game plan for empowering dyslexia and unlocking the extraordinary talents hidden within every dyslexic child. What comes next could completely change how you see learning differences.

# Chapter 2

# Acceptance and Action

*I didn't succeed despite my dyslexia, but because of it. It wasn't my deficit but my advantage. Although there are neurological trade-offs that require that I work creatively [and] smarter in reading, writing and speaking, I would never wish to be any other way than my awesome self. I love being me, regardless of the early challenges I had faced.*

—Scott Sonnon

After receiving a diagnosis and learning how it impacts your child's life, it's time to embrace dyslexia, accept it, and learn how to take early action. You and your child are just at the beginning of your journey. Knowledge enables understanding, but acceptance empowers you to incorporate necessary changes and make forward progress.

Let's pay another visit to Clayton. Good did come out of his first-grade teacher's observation—though she communicated it rudely. After meeting with the teacher, the principal, and Clayton's parents, he underwent a three-day assessment to evaluate his challenges and determine how they affected him. Clayton came away with the diagnosis of dyslexia and began to understand that he was a kinesthetic learner.

According to Kelly Roell of ThoughtCo., "Kinesthetic learners process information best when they are physically engaged during the learning process" (2024). This means that sitting still at a desk in an enclosed room can prevent someone like Clayton from processing the information the instructor is communicating. This is why Clayton stared out the window and chewed on pencils in that first-grade class.

However, Clayton was fortunate to be placed in Mrs. George's second-grade class the following year. What the first-grade teacher had considered a slow or challenged intellect, Mrs. George recognized as a sharp mind that absorbed information through movement and interaction. She specialized in learning needs and brought joy to Clayton at school for the first time. She incorporated worksheets, Lego manipulatives, and creative play in the classroom to keep his body in motion and help his brain take in the material.

In fourth grade, school subjects grew more difficult as Clayton moved away from the basics and into more advanced math, science, grammar, and literature. At this point, he began to see a therapist named Miss Michelle, to whom he attributes much of his understanding of himself. With her guidance, Clayton learned how to work with dyslexia, grow through it, and live happily and successfully with this unique learning style. She helped him grasp that as a kinesthetic learner, he needed to move, talk, write on a whiteboard, or do other physical motions to help him process information. These movements kept his mental gears turning, allowing him to see what was being taught.

Once Clayton understood how his brain worked, he accepted it and turned those unique functions into his greatest strengths. To me, that's another superpower! In my work, I've seen many people in mainstream society who take learning, processing, and acting for granted instead of partnering with their minds to enhance each experience.

In this chapter, we'll examine how accepting a dyslexia diagnosis is the first step toward unlocking your child's full potential. We'll provide tips and strategies that offer insights into intervention techniques and language processing so you can embrace dyslexia and nurture the brilliance of this learning style.

## A Change in Perspective

For too long, society has labelled conditions that diverge from the norm as disabilities, and people diagnosed with these conditions have been treated as if something is inherently wrong with them, as if they're bad simply because they aren't like **"THE REST OF US."**

While there may be fewer people in the world who have dyslexia than those who do not, nothing makes one way of learning better than another. Kids with dyslexia struggle in school because academia caters to the many rather than the few. So, those who learn differently are set apart from their peers and given remedial instruction because most mainstream educators themselves lack an understanding of how to think and learn with a dyslexic brain. Educators, though well-intentioned, often try to give special attention to students with dyslexia, recognizing that traditional teaching methods don't always work. However, they unintentionally set these kids up for ostracism and mockery. As we saw with Clayton's first-grade teacher, even those in authority can push these kids into the spotlight as "retarded." If the teacher sets that example, what's to keep classmates from following their lead?

Acceptance starts with a change in perspective. As I said before, dyslexia is not a disability. Quite the contrary! It's not dis-anything, and it's not even dys-! Both prefixes indicate an abnormality or impairment, but when we teach the dyslexic brain in a way that it best receives information, it excels and can even surpass "normal" minds. *Dis*ability? I think not. Often, it's more like super*ability*.

## *Learning Styles*

Learning styles vary from person to person, even within the realm of "normal." In the 1920s, a group of psychologists developed a model to represent the three main learning styles: visual, auditory, and kinesthetic (VAK). Most people mainly learn through one of the three ways but sometimes combine them depending on the situation.

A few decades later, in 1987, New Zealand educator Neil Fleming split the **"V"** and created a fourth category for reading and writing, expanding the acronym to VARK. Since then, educators have added many variants, but these four remain the core methods of learning:

- **Visual:** Visual learners absorb information best through visuals like diagrams, charts, pictures, videos, movies, and symbols such as circles and arrows—methods that provide a clearer picture than words alone. VARK Learn Limited excludes pictures of reality (moving or still) from this category but includes photos of shapes and symbols, white space, and patterns or drawings of such objects on whiteboards (*VARK Modalities*, n.d.).

- **Auditory:** Auditory learners receive information best from discussions, lectures, music, radio, smartphones, and other devices. They often process information by talking it out. For example, after hearing a lesson, they might explain it back to the teacher in their own words to ensure understanding. They often speak first to organize their thoughts.

- **Reading and writing:** Learners in this category receive information best by making lists, reading textbooks, taking notes, and by repeating words and writing them. They tend to organize thoughts before writing them down as notes or communications.

- **Kinesthetic:** Learners in this category receive information best when they can move their hands or bodies, tangibly experiment with things, or physically participate in hands-on activities. VARK Learn Limited includes videos of objects and activities that provide experiences you can feel, hold, grasp, or taste (*VARK Modalities*, n.d.). For these learners, their own hands-on experiences have more value than learning through others' experiences.

VARK Learn Limited also details two types of learning style combinations or multimodalities.

Based on the situation, the first type involves using any of the four learning styles—visual, auditory, reading/writing, or kinesthetic—. For example, a student might watch a video (visual) to understand a topic, but in a discussion, they may prefer to talk it through (auditory) to reinforce their understanding.

The second multimodality involves using all four learning styles at the same time. For example, a student might watch a video (visual), listen to a lecture (auditory), take notes (reading/writing), and participate in a hands-on activity (kinesthetic) to fully grasp the concept. This combination is often how kids with dyslexia process information, which is why it takes them longer to learn. While it may slow down their learning, it gives them a deeper and more comprehensive understanding of the material (*VARK Modalities*, n.d.).

Both dyslexic and non-dyslexic learners adhere to these learning styles. What sets them apart is how the information is received and processed once it enters the brain.

## *No Deficits, Just Strengths*

Let us learn from Marianne of Homeschooling With Dyslexia (n.d.-a). Seven of her eight children have some form of dyslexia, dysgraphia, dyscalculia, or attention deficit disorder (ADD).

Marianne is a traditional learner and says she never had much difficulty in school, so her children's learning difficulties baffled her. She confesses to feeling flustered by her kids, being impatient with them, and having unrealistic expectations—before learning of and coming to terms with the nuances of dyslexia. She often thought they just needed to try harder or pay closer attention. To make matters worse, people around her judged *her* for her kids' struggles, citing poor parenting, excessive screen time, and foods that negatively affected their mental development. She says that even as she learned about their dyslexia, she still felt the need to "fix" them, get them caught up on the skills they lacked, and make them into traditional learners.

Marianne learned the hard way that resisting acceptance only deepened her frustration.

It took some time, but Marianne eventually broke free from the idea that dyslexia was all about deficits and realized that those so-called "weaknesses" were strengths. In reflecting on this shift in perspective, she quoted graphic designer Madalyne Hymas (n.d.-b):

The way the dyslexic brain works is not bad; it isn't wrong, and it isn't deficient. It's just different. And the difference is not a disability. In fact, the differences in a dyslexic brain bring many unrecognized advantages and are often mislabeled and even maligned.

Hmm, it sounds like what I said in Chapter 1. Please repeat after me (again): **DIFFERENT DOES NOT EQUAL BAD.**

Marianne pulls some points from *The Dyslexic Advantage* by Brock and Fernette Eide to demonstrate that the so-called deficiencies people with dyslexia present are actually super *abilities* (n.d.-b):

- Those with dyslexia have trouble interpreting 2D images, but their gift of thinking and reasoning in 3D compensates for that challenge. This helps them "conceptualize objects or systems and manipulate them in their minds" to gain a more comprehensive understanding. It's much like a landscape designer who might have trouble with a paper plate but can picture the completed project in their mind.

- People with dyslexia easily "make connections between things, see relationships, patterns, and view ideas or objects from different perspectives." Marianne gives the example of an 11-year-old boy with dyslexia who, when asked what comes to mind when hearing the word "cat," took several seconds to ponder it. When his mother interrupted his thought by saying she thought of a kitten, he then told her he wondered if she meant someone named Cat, or if she meant wild animals like tigers and lions, or a mother cat with her babies, or a cuddly kitten, or a high catwalk. The boy connected many things from a single suggestion, whereas his non-dyslexic mom thought only of one.

- Those with dyslexia often think in narratives, connecting mental images from past events to describe the past, present, and future. Though some may struggle with long-term memory, they thrive in these episodic recollections and can hold on to important information almost in cinematic form. Clayton, who I said "could weave words masterfully to compete with *Beowulf* and keep the listener spellbound," views things this way too and describes seeing solutions as if watching a movie in his mind.

- People with dyslexia can sometimes draw from past experiences and project information forward to simulate or anticipate future outcomes. This dynamic reasoning helps them in entrepreneurial endeavours. They are successful because they can stay one step ahead, so the business progresses toward those foreseen goals. In fact, research has shown that about 40% of entrepreneurs have dyslexia (Welch, 2023).

Given these strengths, there are several careers where individuals with dyslexia truly excel. Below is a list of some of these fields, which we'll explore in greater detail in a later chapter:

- Actor

- Architect

- Artist

- Astrophysicist

- Athlete

- Designer

- Engineer

- Marketing, sales, or finance specialist

- Mechanic

- Musician

- Photographer

- Radiologist

- Scientist or researcher

- Software designer

- Woodworker or carpenter

The key is helping your child understand the unique differences between a dyslexic brain and a non-dyslexic brain, while also tailoring learning to their specific strengths. It's about encouraging them to pursue their passions in a way that works best for how they process information. However, this journey depends mainly on accepting their learning style and the support and understanding of those around them.

## Accepting a Dyslexic Mind Requires Two

Dyslexia directly affects the person diagnosed, but it also touches everyone around them. You can be confident, but if those closest to you—your family, teachers, and friends—don't accept that your brain works differently, that you're not "stupid," and that your challenges are just differences, you can still feel isolated. No matter how strong you are, moments of feeling inadequate, rejected, and unloved can still creep in without that support.

Clayton's younger sister, Tatum, never thought much about his dyslexia. Since he was diagnosed at a young age, to her, he was just her fun and goofy brother who happened to learn differently. While Tatum excelled in school, cheerleading, and making friends, she never judged Clayton for struggling in those areas. She figured they had different interests. It wasn't until Clayton's senior year of high school that she understood how much dyslexia affected more than just his reading. Even though it took her a while to fully grasp what he was going through, Tatum never treated him poorly, unlike the bullies—or even one teacher—who did.

With the steady support of those closest to him—his mom, dad, and sister—Clayton thrived in his home environment and carried confidence into the world. It enabled him to tolerate the negative treatment he received from people outside his inner circle. This resilience often develops as people with dyslexia move through different stages of self-acceptance.

Chris Cole of Learning Difference Aotearoa Trust outlined the five states of self-acceptance people with dyslexia go through (2020):

1. **Awareness:** Before diagnosis, many people with dyslexia feel they are different from others, whether academically or socially. We saw this with Vicki, who realized she had dyslexia in her 30s. Though she couldn't pinpoint anything specific, she says she always thought there was something weird about her. Although popular among her peers and very social, she also felt isolated. This feeling comes with knowing you are different but not knowing why.

2. **Labeling:** This is the "why" you are different. Receiving a diagnosis is a catch-22: You're relieved to finally find out the cause of your struggles, especially if it has followed many misdiagnoses. But with that new label comes the risk of others seeing you differently, treating you as if you're somehow less capable. For adults, it's reassuring to finally have an explanation for the challenges they've been hiding or trying to work around for years.

3. **Understanding:** This is a critical stage. Once you receive the label, you will learn what having a learning difficulty means. It can be overwhelming to discover what your brain can and can't do in relation to "normal" people, and it can be confusing to know what kind of help would benefit you. During this stage, you may feel angry that the vague sense of being different or "off" is now confirmed as a reality. It's essential not to camp out in negativity but to understand your capabilities, learn how you learn, and make adjustments to help you grow and not stagnate in "why me" or, worse, "poor me."

4. **Compartmentalization:** As you move through the previous stage, you'll start to understand dyslexia and its impact on your life. You'll begin to see it as a difference rather than a disability. You'll recognize your strengths and how this difference has helped you face specific challenges. Over time, you'll notice areas where dyslexia has given you an advantage over those without it. You'll also become more confident in advocating for yourself. While certain situations may still cause frustration, you'll start to understand why you feel that way. As you gain insight into how your brain processes information, you'll find new ways to approach things that work best for you. Clayton credits his therapist, Miss Michelle, for teaching him about himself and helping him know how his brain works. With this new insight, he can now approach tasks in *his own way* rather than relying on traditional methods designed for non-dyslexic learners, which

has been incredibly freeing.

5. **Transformation:** The fifth and final stage occurs when you fully accept dyslexia. You've become aware of it, attached a name to it, understood it, and realized you can thrive with it! Now, with a positive perspective, you can advocate for yourself. You may have to navigate social stigma; in some situations, you may only have the support of those closest to you. Arriving at self-acceptance isn't an easy path, but it is a reachable destination.

Regardless of their age—even if they're adults—your child may need some help coming to terms with their diagnosis. Here are five ways you can help them:

- **Try not to catastrophize:** Children are little sponges; they pick up the emotions of the people around them and are especially attuned to Mom's and Dad's. If you panic and see only the negatives, they will, too; however, if you provide love, support, and encouragement with positivity, you will empower them to live life to the fullest.

- **Learn all you can:** Just like the person diagnosed needs to learn about dyslexia, you must also do so. You are your child's strongest supporter, and you need to understand what this learning difference is and what your child experiences on a daily basis. They need you to help them know themselves, and they need your patience. Start by researching effective treatments, exploring lifestyle changes that could support them, and providing them with a strong foundation. This might involve incorporating tools like audiobooks for reading, setting up a quiet, structured study space, and offering consistent encouragement to build their confidence in facing future challenges.

- **Don't make your child talk if they're not ready:** As your child's parent, you are naturally concerned about the implications of their dyslexia diagnosis and how it will affect them. While you may feel powerless, it's important to remember they are the ones who are living with it, and they are probably going through a lot of intense emotions. They, of course, need to understand dyslexia and how the diagnosis impacts their life, but don't force them to talk about it. That will only overwhelm them and stress them out more. Give them time to let things settle. If they approach you, don't turn them away, but otherwise, wait until they're ready.

- **Meet your child wherever they are on their journey:** Everyone adjusts to things at a different pace. Your child may have already processed the what and the why and is ready to embrace the new. Meet them wherever they are on their journey. If they've reached a point of understanding and acceptance before you have, follow their lead. Learn from their acceptance, and let them guide you to the same level. If they're struggling with any step, be patient and encouraging, and love them through it.

- **Build your support network:** It's easy to feel like you're all alone on this journey and that nobody understands what you're going through. While you're still learning and your family is adjusting, seek support. Search for online forums, check if your local church offers networking groups, and ask your child's therapist or teacher for recommendations on where you can find support—not just for your child, but for you as a parent. You're on this journey with them, and neither one of you is travelling solo. Others have walked the same path as you and your child, ready to help you find your footing and show you the bright possibilities ahead.

As mentioned in that last point, this is a new experience for you, too, and you're on this journey with your child. Here are some things you can do to help yourself accept and cope with your child's diagnosis:

- **Permit yourself to feel what you're feeling:** This is big, new, messy, and overwhelming. You might feel angry, heartbroken, frustrated, or completely lost. That's the reality right now, and it's okay to feel like this. Yes, your child is looking to you for support and encouragement, but you don't have to pretend you're okay with everything. Be honest with yourself—if you need a moment, take it. Step away, cry if you need to, and allow yourself to feel. Opening up to someone you trust or journaling your emotions can also help you process everything. It's okay not to have all the answers right now.

- **Prioritize your relationship with your spouse and other children:** It is easy to get caught up in the demands of a new diagnosis and unintentionally neglect other relationships. Be sure to prioritize your loved ones—schedule regular date nights with your partner, set aside time to catch up with friends or plan family activities that don't revolve around the diagnosis.

- **Don't neglect yourself:** As mentioned above, it's easy to get so caught up in the diagnosis that your relationships start to suffer, including the one with yourself. Don't bottle up your emotions or feel like you must be your family's constant source of strength. It's essential to take care of your own needs, too. Talk to friends and family, join support groups, and don't hesitate to seek counselling if needed. Make time for activities you enjoy, and schedule them into your calendar—then make sure you keep those appointments for yourself.

- **Go at your own pace:** A dyslexia diagnosis is significant, and there's a lot to absorb. Along with managing your child's and your own emotions, you might feel pressure to quickly learn everything to support your child. But remember, you won't master it all overnight. Take your time, learn at your own pace, and ask questions. It's perfectly fine if you don't understand everything right away.

- **Limit your online research:** The internet offers a wealth of information, but not all of it is accurate.

When researching, limit yourself to studying only legitimate, trustworthy resources. Set a timer for the time you spend online so you don't overwhelm yourself or become consumed by too much information.

## *Taking Action*

The earlier you accept and address dyslexia, the better. Every school subject involves reading, and as your child moves up in grade levels, the terms become more advanced and the work more complex. Without a proper diagnosis and treatment, the chances of falling behind and struggling in school increase each year. Acting early can help prevent this.

Early intervention gives your child the tools to manage dyslexia from the start. It allows them to understand their learning style, build confidence, and avoid the frustration of feeling like they're "bad at school." By addressing challenges early, they're less likely to develop a negative self-image and more likely to feel capable and empowered in their learning journey. According to GoLexic, "Studies find that when the intervention takes place between the ages of 6 and 9, about 90% of children will be able to achieve grade-level reading abilities. This number drops to 25% when intervention is delayed beyond age 9" (*Reading Comprehension*, 2023).

The reading skills of children with dyslexia do not automatically progress and mature; explicit language decoding and encoding skills are essential for them to develop strong reading fluency. Here are some effective approaches:

- Multisensory activities involving visual, auditory, kinesthetic, and tactile associations

- Frequent lessons presented in brief sessions

- Guided practice

- One-on-one or small-group instruction

- Subject-based intervention in the following areas:

  - *Reading*: Structured phonics programs are most effective.

  - *Spelling:* This includes a systematic focus on phonics, letter, word, and number sound awareness, spelling, vocabulary, grammar, memory skills, and an understanding of how one learns.

  - *Writing:* Children receive explicit instruction in speaking and reading comprehension skills, as well as studying sentence structure and the purpose of writing.

  - *Mathematics*: Special emphasis is given to number sense, math facts, problem-solving techniques, counting strategies, and the language used in mathematics.

- Strengths-based teaching: This method focuses on what the child can do rather than what needs to be corrected. Children are encouraged to use their strengths to help compensate for weaker areas. For instance, a child might learn morphemic spelling by breaking down the word "preview" into "pre-" (meaning before) and "view" (meaning to see). By understanding the meaning of each part, spelling becomes easier and more intuitive.

Though dyslexia is not something that can or needs to be "fixed," remedial interventions can sometimes be effective. At Carroll School in Massachusetts, specialists found that combining strengths-based approaches with remedial systems can lead to even better outcomes. They collaborated with neuroscientists John Gabrieli and Eric Falke to develop Targeted Cognitive Intervention (TCI). This approach aims to "strengthen cognitive skills and their underlying pathways to the brain" through individualized instruction by improving the speed and efficiency of communication between brain regions responsible for receiving, interpreting, and processing written language (Sheehan & Wilkins, 2019). They identified the students' weakest areas and designed a customized curriculum for each student's greatest need. Data analysis revealed that cognitive growth drives academic progress. In effect, TCI strengthens the reading network in the dyslexic brain. This way, strengths and perceived weaknesses can be dealt with together, improving capabilities.

## To Understand a Different Language

Ever tried talking to someone in a foreign country and gotten nowhere? Maybe you tossed out a few English words, hoping they'd recognize them, or butchered a phrase in their language—only to be met with a blank stare, like you just asked them to explain quantum physics! You probably felt lost, like no one spoke your language. Now, picture living in a world where that's your everyday experience—where only you understand how you think and communicate.

That's how many people with dyslexia feel.

Recall from the introduction that when Clayton was little and first learning printed letters, he might see the letter "B" on a flashcard but fail to recognize it when it cycled through again. His mom would get frustrated that it *seemed like* he couldn't remember the letter when, in reality, "B" had morphed, flipped, or danced into some other image inside his mind. Clayton didn't realize what was happening, so he didn't tell his mom or anyone else. To him, he just saw a different letter or shape each time.

Clayton was already showing signs of one of his special abilities: his unique internal language. The problem? No one else could understand it but him.

Orthography is the process of representing sounds by written symbols. For example, the sound /k/ can be represented by the letter "C" in "cat" or "K" in "kite." All languages utilize this process, an integral component of reading acquisition. Dyslexia often causes difficulties with orthography, particularly in alphabet-based languages like English, where matching sounds to letters can be incredibly challenging. Dyslexia also occurs in other languages; however, the severity depends on what researchers call the transparency of the grapheme-phoneme relationship (Borleffs et al., 2019).

In other words, it's easy to match letters to sounds in languages like Spanish, Italian, Finnish, and Indonesian because the relationship is consistent and predictable.

FOR EXAMPLE, IN SPANISH, THE LETTER **"E"** IS ALWAYS PRONOUNCED AS **/E/,** LIKE IN **"ELEPHANTE,"** AND THE LETTER "S" CONSISTENTLY REPRESENTS THE **/S/** SOUND, AS IN **"SOL."**

This straightforward pattern makes connecting written letters with their corresponding sounds easier. However, English and Danish are opaque because the letters and their corresponding sounds are extremely variable.

FOR EXAMPLE, THE **"K"** SOUND IN ENGLISH CAN BE REPRESENTED BY THE LETTERS **"K"** AND **"C,"** THE BLENDS "CK" AND **"CH,"** AND EVEN A **"QUEUE"** COMBINATION.

If a child hasn't encountered words with varied spellings in their vocabulary, they can't sound them out phonetically. So, even if they recognize and process the letters correctly, they may still struggle to match them with the right sounds.

Phonology isn't the only determining factor in reading struggles. Deficits in the way the brain processes visual motion, delays in making decisions based on what you perceive visually, cognitive functions that differ from what is considered the norm, extent of linguistic capabilities, and competency of non-sensory mechanisms can contribute to the development of dyslexia as well and indicate a reduced ability to encode and integrate visual information (O'Brien & Yeatman, 2020). Research also shows children who are eventually diagnosed with dyslexia may have had initial trouble learning to speak. It can be hard to notice because "baby talk" can sometimes be indiscernible. These children were likely on the lower end of formative speech or delayed learning to talk (Price et al., 2021).

It's essential to consider these factors as you appropriately adapt interventions to suit your child's needs.

\*\*\*

# Summary

Accepting a dyslexia diagnosis is not just about school re-sults; school is only for a few years. Adulthood—supporting yourself and your family—is what happens beyond. A typical, natural lifespan that's not cut short by outside factors lasts an average of 76 years for women and 71 for men (*Life Expectancy*, n.d.). That's a good 50+ years your child will have to navigate using a mind that receives and processes infor-mation differently than most of the world's population. Give them a good chance for success by accepting and helping them reach acceptance now.

As we continue, we'll explore the MORE framework, begin-ning with the first of dyslexia's hidden strengths: multifac-eted ingenuity. Join us as we explore how children with dyslexia tackle challenges in creative and unexpected ways. How might their unique problem-solving abilities reshape the way we approach learning and creativity?

# Part 2: The Strengths of Dyslexic Thinking

Chapter 3

# Strength #1 Multifaceted Ingenuity

*My 9-year-old daughter's dyslexia makes her feel both confident and self-conscious. She likes having a 'different' brain that loves colour and creativity.*

—Lyn Pollard

As you've been learning, there's *more* to dyslexia than meets the eye. In this chapter, we'll explore the first part of the MORE framework: multifaceted ingenuity.

The term "multifaceted" describes something with many sides—like a diamond unearthed from the rough, meticulously shaped and polished, with each facet gleaming, sending light dancing across its surface like the twinkle of distant stars. Its sharp edges catch the light, scattering a spectrum of colours that shine within the stone and outward for all to see. With 70 facets, the radiant cut sparkles with a brilliance unmatched, its fiery glow captivating anyone who sees it. What if ingenuity—cleverness, inventiveness—had the cuts and polish of a radiant-cut diamond?

Many sides and many angles provide many opportunities for brilliance to shine.

Children with dyslexia possess multifaceted ingenuity, and their learning and processing methods involve multiple aspects. When you learn to recognize and celebrate this, you'll begin to see the diverse ways children with dyslexia think and perceive the world.

## Dyslexic Minds Have An Even MORE Multifaceted Ingenuity

A facet can be a planed surface like a radiant diamond or one of many definable subject aspects, like problem-solving. If a subject or object has many facets, it is fascinating and desirable. When you combine that concept with the ingenious skills of devising and designing extraordinary approaches to challenges, you develop a sophisticated, creative, and exceptional individual.

In simple terms, intelligence + intuition = multifaceted ingenuity. This strength refers to the ability to approach challenges or problems from various angles, utilizing diverse skills, perspectives, and resources to find innovative solutions. It involves adaptability and versatility and requires the competence to draw upon multiple talents and insights to address complex issues or tasks.

The best way to understand multifaceted ingenuity is to look at Clayton's story once more.

Clayton's mind couldn't properly receive instructions at school if he was confined to a desk and forced to sit still. He would lose focus and stop paying attention. It gave his teachers and classmates the impression he was slow, and until he learned how his brain worked, he too struggled to understand *why he struggled to understand.* It turned out he learned differently than most of the other students. He began to thrive once he grasped that physical motion engaged his mind and helped knowledge sink in.

Tom, Clayton's dad, read bedtime Bible stories to Clayton when he was little, and they'd act them out. Clayton struggled to interpret the letters on the page, but his vivid internal vision allowed him to understand the lesson and picture the characters and events in his mind. When his dad read about the shepherd boy David and the giant soldier Goliath, Clayton felt as if he were standing in the valley between them, watching David hurl the stone and seeing Goliath fall to his end. Clayton describes his problem-solving techniques similarly—he visualizes the entire process, from start to finish, playing them out in his mind.

Clayton discovered his differences had advantages as he advanced through school and into adulthood! They have pushed him to use nontraditional problem-solving abilities and look for solutions where most people wouldn't think to go. Clayton has a natural gift for speaking, but when he puts his thoughts into writing, he finds it challenging to express them clearly. When breaking down sentences and paragraphs, Clayton orates his reports aloud, allowing him to place punctuation where it belongs. This same ability to process information verbally extends to problem-solving. He often comes up with multiple solutions to a problem by visualizing the outcome without overthinking or overanalyzing. *That* is multifaceted ingenuity.

## Multifaceted Ingenuity in the Real World

Spain's *Instituto de Empresa*, or IE University, calls ingenuity humans' "secret sauce." IE emphasizes that, as a species, we excel at ingenuity—the ability to solve problems creatively—which is driven by three key components: communication, collaboration, and innovation. In further discussion, they declare human ingenuity as the most strategic asset you can have in an entity or organization. It's a popular buzzword among significant corporations, comes up in climate change discussions, and it—along with judgment and creativity—is deemed by one of the world's "Big Four" accounting firms, Ernst & Young Global Limited (EY), as a driver for innovation in new technology (*Human Ingenuity*, 2017).

It may seem strange to suggest that people with dyslexia are instrumental in the first aspect of ingenuity—communication—when they struggle with it the most. Collaboration, another facet, could also be a hindrance as it directly involves communication with partners, coworkers, and peers. Innovation, however, balances out the discussion.

Remember how I mentioned that Clayton *sees* solutions in his mind? That's a result of his multifaceted ingenuity. It's how he incorporates communication, collaboration, and innovation into an effective system to utilize "sets of instructions that tell [him] how to arrange the constituent parts of [the] physical and social worlds in ways that help [him] achieve [his] goals" (Homer-Dixon, as cited in *Human Ingenuity*, 2017). Humans are natural problem solvers, but people with dyslexia—thanks to their multifaceted ingenuity—often have an advantage over those without it.

When Clayton was around 10 or 12, his parents had their pool deck resurfaced. A layer of dust settled on the water, leaving a stubborn film across the surface. Tom and Vicki tried everything to remove it. First, they ran the pool vacuum—yeah, that did absolutely nothing. Next, they tried a chemical treatment—no luck. Then, they attempted skimming it with a big net—still nothing. Desperate for a solution, Tom turned to the internet and found an idea: toss 100 tennis balls into the pool. The theory? The felt would soak up the dust. The result? A pool full of soggy tennis balls and not a speck of dust removed.

As Tom watched the balls *not* remove the dust, Clayton walked outside to see what his dad was up to. He took one look and immediately *saw* the solution in his mind. He said, "Dad, just flood the pool." Now, Tom was an intelligent man, but he stood there dumbfounded. Clayton said, "Yeah. Just fill the water till it overflows, and that layer of film on top will run right out with it." It worked like a charm! Once it all flowed out, Tom ran over to Clayton, picked him up in a big bear hug, and threw him in the pool!

Clayton recalls his dad telling and retelling that story many times over the years, and never once did Tom's amazement diminish. He never stopped being astonished by his son's problem-solving superpowers.

As you can see, Clayton's story is a perfect example of how dyslexia can enhance problem-solving through multifaceted ingenuity, turning challenges into opportunities.

Let's explore how this unique ability helps the dyslexic mind thrive in even the most complex situations.

### *How Multifaceted Ingenuity Helps the Dyslexic Mind Thrive*

On the surface, multifaceted ingenuity seems complicated. With so many different sides, options, and perspectives seemingly swirling in their mind, how can a child with dyslexia benefit from it all? How does it not confuse them or add to their existing frustrations? Well, the dyslexic mind can come up with, assess, and decide on solutions almost immediately; that's how. And even when they *do* encounter a difficult situation, they put in the extra effort and "work a little bit harder than the other kids to get the same result," as Jay Leno's mother once told him, reflecting on his experience with dyslexia (Crockett, n.d.).

As a young boy, Jay Leno developed a unique view of his dyslexia. He knew that many others talked about "struggling" in school and described it as a "hardship," but he didn't mind working harder. He even embraced his low self-esteem, explaining;

IF YOU DON'T THINK YOU'RE THE SMARTEST PERSON IN THE
ROOM AND YOU THINK YOU'RE GOING TO HAVE TO WORK A
LITTLE HARDER AND PUT A LITTLE MORE TIME INTO IT TO GET
WHAT EVERYBODY ELSE DOES, YOU CAN ACTUALLY DO QUITE
WELL (LENO, AS CITED IN CROCKETT, N.D.).

Leno says that when he was younger, he would write someone a letter while simultaneously reciting the Pledge of Alle-
giance to strengthen his communication abilities. While performing stand-up comedy, he'd be saying his bit, and at the
same time, "with the other side of [his] brain," he'd be thinking about what he could say about an audience member he
noticed. As a late-night TV host, he preferred to use cue cards
instead of teleprompters because he could "see the whole
thing at once... [and] put it in [his] own words." He describes
himself as a visual thinker, learning best by watching a video
tutorial rather than reading instructions, which coincides
with the VARK definition we explored in Chapter 2. Over time,
Leno "discovered that being a little bit different actually sets
you aside in show business; it makes you special. You always
try to turn your negative into a positive" (Leno, as cited in
Crockett, n.d.).

Leno's story illustrates how dyslexia, rather than being a setback, can shape extraordinary abilities and creative thinking.
His willingness to embrace hard work and a different way of
seeing the world helped him succeed.

Now, let's consider how the right environment and encouragement can foster a child's innate desire to learn and explore.

## How to Harness This Strength

Children have an innate desire to learn. They naturally want to know about what they see around them—plants, animals, sounds, and structures. When placed in an environment that stimulates their minds and allows them the freedom to explore it, children can be intuitive and lead themselves along the path to knowledge and discovery. But they need your support and encouragement as they learn to recognize those internal drives.

One approach to childhood development called "Theory-Theory" compares children to scientists, who devise their own theories of understanding as they encounter and interact with the world around them. As they grow, they essentially conduct experiments to test and assess their conclusions, making modifications as necessary. This early establishment of knowledge becomes the basis of their intuition, building self-esteem, developing independent thinking, and sharpening problem-solving skills (Spalding, 2020).

Children who've been diagnosed with dyslexia share eight common strengths, according to Ron Davis of Davis Dyslexia Association International (2010):

- The physical manner by which their brains receive information creates alternate perceptions, so letters, words, and numbers look different to them than they appear on paper.

- Most are visual thinkers who see pictures in their minds instead of hearing words.

- They have a stronger curiosity than their peers.

- Many have very vivid imaginations.

- They have an acute awareness of the environment.

- They use all their senses to perceive things and think multi-dimensionally.

- They often experienced their thoughts as a reality.

- They are incredibly insightful and highly intuitive.

Davis, who established his unique learning program at the age of 38 after discovering a way to overcome symptoms of his severe dyslexia, calls these eight traits *natural abilities*, *gifts*, and *talents* (2010). He says that when they are supported and encouraged, these characteristics can lead to exceptional creative skills and above-average intelligence.

# Summary

This chapter highlights the multifaceted ingenuity of individuals with dyslexia, showing how their unique strengths allow them to approach challenges creatively and find solutions that others may overlook.

Clayton's story illustrates how this extraordinary strength helps him solve problems in nontraditional ways and find solutions where most people wouldn't think to go. Jay Leno's experiences further demonstrated multifaceted ingenuity by the way he learned to embrace his challenges and discover novel methods of conveying his thoughts.

It's crucial to allow children with dyslexia to explore the world around them, who they are, how their brains function, and what natural abilities, gifts, and talents they possess *because of* their dyslexia.

The next chapter will consider the second aspect of **MORE: Out-of-the-box Thinking.** Multifaceted ingenuity naturally leads to this exceptional cognitive strength by making limitations practically invisible to dyslexic minds and allowing them to go beyond the borders imposed by traditional ideation to discover new and innovative possibilities.

# Your Turn to Write!

*It shouldn't matter how slowly a child learns. What matters is that we encourage them to never stop trying.*

—Robert J. Meehan

You've made it this far, which either means you're deeply committed or just as stubbornly optimistic as the rest of us. So, let's talk about reviews. Before the eye roll, hear me out.

This book wasn't just written to sit on a shelf; it's here to promote change. Your review is what helps broaden the world's perspective on dyslexia, nudging others to step up with compassion, education, and support for those who need it most.

So, if you're up for making someone's day, go ahead—scan the code or go to the following link, and drop a few words. It will only take you a minute or two!

 Note: If the QR code doesn't work, please visit the Amazon marketplace where you purchased the book. Scroll to the bottom of the book's product page and click on **'Write a customer review'** to leave your feedback manually.

You've made a difference that's louder than a phonics lesson—*thank you!*

# Chapter 4

# Strength #2 Outside-the-Box Thinking

*Dyslexic kids are creative, 'outside-the-box' thinkers. They have to be because they don't see or solve problems the same way other kids do.*

—Rick Riordan

One of the most notable abilities of people with dyslexia is thinking differently from the crowd. We consider this the second of the MORE strengths: outside-the-box thinking.

In this chapter, we'll explore the incredible benefits of out-of-the-box thinking children with dyslexia often possess. We'll explore how these strengths become evident and how to maximize them. This way, you can better understand your dyslexic learners' cognitive profiles and help them recognize and appreciate this aspect of themselves. We'll also provide actionable strategies to help your child leverage these abilities in academic and personal settings.

## Thinking Outside the Box

Let's revisit Christian, who struggled with reading in school. His teachers were frustrated, and his classmates sometimes teased him. However, one day, Christian surprised everyone. The teacher assigned the class to present an original story. Instead of writing it out, Christian created a beautiful mural that told the tale of a superhero with powers rooted in kindness and cleverness. This showed his teacher and classmates that he was indeed capable of communicating deep emotions and thoughts, giving them a glimpse of his intellectual abilities, which had previously been considered compromised.

Christian's out-of-the-box thinking allowed him to turn what felt like a disadvantage in reading into a fantastic visual story. This moment of success was pivotal for him as it demonstrated that he could express his ideas in ways that went beyond traditional learning.

Out-of-the-box thinking refers to the ability to approach problems in new and creative ways. It involves innovative thinking that goes beyond the standard methods. It is an extension of the multifaceted ingenuity discussed in the previous chapter. Many learners with dyslexia possess a talent for visual thinking, meaning they can see things from unique angles. They may grasp concepts better through images and symbols rather than through text. This skill can be nurtured by encouraging creative expressions, such as drawing, building, or even storytelling in alternative formats.

Here are a few actionable strategies for fostering this type of thinking:

1. **Encourage using visual aids**: Diagrams, charts, and other visual tools can help them process information better. For example, if they struggle to understand a math concept, it might make more sense to them if they draw it out visually.

2. **Promote hands-on learning**: Learning by doing can be incredibly effective for dyslexic thinkers. Doing simple science experiments or building models can reinforce concepts while allowing for exploration and creativity.

3. **Value different perspectives**: Open discussions in which diverse ideas are shared in classrooms or group settings can stimulate out-of-the-box thinking. Group brainstorming sessions can lead to innovative solutions that might not be discovered through conventional means.

4. **Incorporate storytelling**: Using storytelling as a teaching tool can engage dyslexic learners, just like Clayton and his dad did when Clayton was young. Children with dyslexia can build narratives around subjects they're learning about, making the material more relatable and memorable. Clayton described it as viewing a movie in his mind; because he could see

it, he could understand it, whereas if he had only jumbled letters on a page, the process of making sense of the text would have been much less enjoyable and had much less of an impact on him.

Beyond educational settings, these strategies can also be integrated into everyday life. Recognizing and celebrating these strengths can boost your child's confidence and self-esteem. Here are some practical ways to do this:

- **Celebrate creativity**: Acknowledge your child's creative efforts in whatever form they take. Whether it's a drawing, reciting a poem, or coming up with an idea during play, show appreciation to help them feel valued.

- **Create a safe space for ideas:** Encourage children to share their ideas without judgment. This can be done through open discussions at home where they feel comfortable expressing their thoughts, even unconventional ones.

- **Introduce problem-solving games**: Engage them in games that require strategy and creative thinking, such as puzzles or outdoor challenges, to enhance their problem-solving skills in an entertaining way.

For more tools and strategies to foster self-esteem and confidence don't forget to download the free bonus bundle I put together for you. Simply scan the QR code below:

Children with dyslexia often tend towards insecurity because they know very well—and it's frequently pointed out to them in the classroom and school hallways—that they are different. This can make them hesitant to express their creative nature, even if those ideas might be world-changing. Your affirmation of your child's gifts gives them courage and empowers them to speak up and participate with firm self-assurance.

Providing opportunities for out-of-the-box thinking nurtures their strengths and validates a different way of processing the world, preparing them for future success. Real-world scenarios often require innovative solutions. For example, maybe the standard business plan isn't working, and a new approach is needed. Or perhaps an office space needs to be expanded without increasing the building's size. Individuals with dyslexia are frequently well-equipped to tackle such challenges; you just have to give them a chance.

It's also essential to connect these creative strengths to specific academic subjects. For example, in science, students with dyslexia can benefit from learning through observation and experimentation rather than memorization. Science fairs are great platforms for them to showcase their creative projects and reinforce the idea that their unique approach can lead to compelling scientific conclusions.

In language arts, efforts to develop storytelling skills can revolutionize how children with dyslexia engage with reading and writing. Instead of adhering to traditional formats, students can be encouraged to create comic strips, write dialogues, or use digital storytelling apps for multimedia presentations. In the real world, this goes beyond professional writing and can be applied on a more intimate individual scale. Recall from Chapter 1 how Clayton's storytelling abilities helped him to connect with his employees and improve morale in the office. As a result, employee performance and productivity also trended upward.

Always remember that every child is different. Some may excel in visual arts, while others struggle to solve logical puzzles or understand spatial relationships. The key is to observe their interests and talents and guide them toward activities that align with those strengths.

Because educators have such a vital role in cultivating these unique skills, schools and other educational organizations should provide training programs for their teachers. Clayton's parents were fortunate to be in a position to assist his school. However, many public districts in the United States and education systems worldwide do little to nothing to help instructors understand dyslexia or enable them to help these children develop their creative thinking skills. Encourage your child's school system to look into one or more of the available programs, such as those listed below:

- **Academy of Orton-Gillingham Practitioners and Educators (AOGPE)**: ortonacademy.org/training-certification/individual-certification

- **AIM Institute for Learning and Research**: institute.aimpa.org

- **The APPLE Group for Dyslexia:** applegroupdyslexia.com

- **Dyslexia Training Institute**: dyslexiatraininginstitute.org

- **The International Multisensory Structured Language Education Council (IMSLEC):** imslec.org/directory.asp?action=accredited

- **Step-by-Step Learning/MGT Consulting**: mgtconsulting.ac-page.com/stepbysteplearning

- **Wilson Language Training (WLT)**: wilsonlanguage.com

NOTE: THE INTERNATIONAL DYSLEXIA ORGANIZATION WEBSITE HAS A COMPREHENSIVE LIST OF TEACHER TRAINING PROGRAMS AT .

Training teachers can make a significant difference by shifting the focus from simply helping students manage their challenges to actively fostering their strengths. Schools could then incorporate flexible lesson plans and allow students to demonstrate their knowledge in various formats that cater to their unique learning styles.

The road may not always be smooth, but with the proper support and strategies, out-of-the-box thinking can lead to extraordinary achievements.

# MORE Dyslexic Minds Think Outside the Box

Thinking outside the box is a valuable skill but often comes with a cost. Clayton explains that his mind constantly runs through many possible solutions to a problem, quickly assessing and narrowing them down to find the best one. This ability to see multiple options keeps his brain in constant motion; it's *always* trying to solve *all* the problems. Clayton has never slept well because his mind has difficulty shutting down and resting. Even as a young child, his mind churned, and he suffered restless sleep. He was known to knock on his parents' bedroom door late at night—not because of a nightmare, but because he couldn't fall asleep.

So much thinking does not result from overthinking, where you endlessly dwell on a topic until it drains you. Instead, dyslexic thinking is a form of constant problem-solving, always searching for solutions. It's considering and discovering new ways of doing things that take the humdrum and malfunction out of challenges they don't even know exist. This allows children with dyslexia to reach beyond the limits of the so-called "box" and devise unconventional approaches.

Several important skills are involved in outside-the-box thinking:

- **Big-picture thinking:** This means seeing how a sit-

uation's smaller parts fit together to create a larg-
er whole. For example, when planning a community
event, a big-picture thinker will consider the event's
logistics, how it will impact the community, how it will
bring people together, and how it aligns with community goals. A child with dyslexia may look at their
messy bedroom and see the neat, tidy, and organized
result by doing the small tasks to clean it up.

- **Problem-solving:** This is the ability to find solutions
to different challenges. A person who excels in problem-solving will often approach a difficult situation by
breaking it down into smaller parts and looking for
creative ways to address each part. For example, if a
team faces a tight project deadline, a problem-solver
might suggest new methods to streamline processes
or delegate tasks more effectively. Recall Clayton's
"flood-the-pool" solution to removing the film from
the water's surface. He broke the issue down to its
most fundamental problem and saw the clear answer
in his mind.

- **Critical thinking**: Critical thinking involves analyzing information, questioning assumptions, evaluating evidence, and considering alternative viewpoints.
This approach helps people make informed decisions
rather than just accepting things at face value. For
instance, in a discussion about a new policy at work,
a critical thinker will explore potential weaknesses
and offer suggestions for improvement. Rote memorization might not work for a student with dyslexia,

but evaluating evidence and exploring options can help them see that a hands-on approach is a more effective way for them to learn.

- **Abstract thinking:** This is the ability to think about concepts and ideas that are not directly tied to physical objects. People who think abstractly might connect unrelated ideas to create a new product or service. For example, a designer might take inspiration from nature to create a new type of useful and environmentally friendly packaging. As mentioned above, the mind of a child with dyslexia is often cranking away on its own, looking for solutions to problems they don't even know exist. This demonstrates an unconscious abstract thought.

- **Observation**: Good observers notice details that others might overlook. This skill allows individuals to gather insights and understand situations on a deeper level. For instance, a marketer may carefully observe consumer behaviour to identify trends that can inform future campaigns. They can find innovative ways to engage their audience by paying attention to what is happening. Because their mind is constantly at work, a child with dyslexia excels at taking in what's happening around them. They internalize it and process it to come to a clear understanding of the situation.

Though his brain is in constant motion, Clayton feels he's solving problems, even while sleeping. He says he also filters information rapidly to keep up with the myriad of considerations swirling through his mind. He breaks down barriers and connects more efficiently and effectively with others by narrowing his focus.

## Build a New Box

Steve Jobs was known for encouraging his team to think differently when creating new products. When designing the iPhone, he challenged them to imagine what the future of communication could look like. This mindset led to the development of technology that revolutionized the industry. He and his team developed something new and innovative, solving several problems with one handy gadget. A work environment conducive to out-of-the-box thinking by inviting it, celebrating it, and thriving in it is a career path your child should consider. They may not create the gadget to replace the iPhone, but they could resolve overcrowding in an inner-city school district, develop the next great family board game, or design a device that keeps ships from sinking.

On more minor everyday scales, your child's mind is thinking, their internal gears are spinning, and they're solving many problems by taking a different perspective and braving a nontraditional approach. Many teachers have embraced creative methods to make learning more engaging for learners with dyslexia. For instance, some educators assign project-based learning instead of giving traditional lectures. This allows students to work on real-world problems by encouraging them to collaborate, communicate, and think outside the box. Students might team up to create a presentation on a local issue, which makes their learning more relevant and relatable.

## The Advantages of Thinking Outside the Box

The enhanced creativity and resourceful problem-solving of people with dyslexia boost their ability to generate innovative solutions that might not be immediately obvious. Let's take a look at some advantages of outside-the-box thinking:

- **It fosters innovation**: When people feel free to explore new ideas—or, in the case of the dyslexic mind, are unable to prevent new ideas from popping into their heads—they can develop products and services that meet the needs of society. I've read story after story of adults who overcame challenges brought on by their dyslexia by developing methods that help them work with it instead of trying to fix it or learn according to ineffective systems. Ron Davis, whom we mentioned in the previous chapter, established the Davis Dyslexia Association International as a global organization designed to use methods he developed that helped him overcome challenges caused by dyslexia. Though he's now retired, his work continues to benefit thousands of people worldwide.

- **It enhances adaptability:** Those thinking outside traditional frameworks are better equipped to handle unexpected challenges in a rapidly changing world. For example, during the COVID-19 pandemic, companies that quickly adapted their operations to remote work found new ways to connect with their customers, allowing them to survive and even thrive during difficult times. Because the dyslexic mind sees beyond limitations, children and adults with dyslexia are more adept at adapting.

- **It encourages collaboration:** When people from different backgrounds share their unique perspectives, they spark creativity. Collaborative teams often find solutions more effectively because they combine various viewpoints and experiences. A child or adult with dyslexia will bring creative ideas to the table, but they can also skillfully take the suggestions of others and flesh them out.

## Why Dyslexic Minds Excel

Individuals with dyslexia approach tasks in nonlinear ways and often rely on creativity to overcome obstacles. For example, a child with dyslexia might struggle with traditional reading tasks but excel in puppet play, where they can demonstrate their understanding of the reading material through physical action. The box says, "Sit and stare at words on the page until they make sense," but tear down those walls, and authentic learning will set in.

Please encourage your child and nurture their potential. Don't solely focus on traditional academic achievements but celebrate their unique talents, recognize them, and foster them. With encouragement, kids like Christian, who struggle with words on the page but can express their ideas through art, can develop self-confidence and a lifelong love of learning.

## Out-of-the-Box Thinking in the Real World

Richard Branson, founder of the Virgin Group, struggled with dyslexia throughout his school years, which made learning difficult. However, he developed strong out-of-the-box thinking and problem-solving skills that have helped him build a global brand. Branson often emphasizes the importance of surrounding himself with talented individuals who complement his skills. His journey shows that with creativity and determination, those with dyslexia can achieve remarkable things.

Steven Spielberg, one of the most well-known filmmakers in history, faced challenges during his childhood due to dyslexia and found conventional education difficult. However, his unique perspective and innovative storytelling abilities led him to become a pioneer in the film industry. His movies often break traditional narrative structures and showcase his creativity. Spielberg's success underlines how thinking differently can lead to groundbreaking work in any field.

These success stories demonstrate that overcoming challenges is essential to personal growth. Children with dyslexia can learn to embrace their struggles as opportunities. Please encourage them to pursue interests that excite them and talk to them freely about their thoughts and ideas. Help build their confidence in their unique abilities to develop resilience and creativity, leading to discovering new talents and strengths.

## *Reflecting on Individual Strengths*

According to Disney historian Jim Korkis, Walt Disney discouraged his employees from thinking outside the box:

> TODAY, PEOPLE TALK ABOUT "THINKING OUTSIDE THE BOX,"
> BUT WALT WOULD SAY, "NO! DON'T THINK OUTSIDE THE BOX!
> ONCE YOU SAY THAT, YOU'VE ESTABLISHED THAT THERE IS A
> BOX." WALT WOULD REFUSE TO ACCEPT THE EXISTENCE OF A
> BOX (KORKIS, AS QUOTED IN TAYLOR, 2017).

Boxes are confining. They're great for storing things, but they have limits. They can only hold so much. Walt wasn't telling people not to be creative, innovate, or think big; on the contrary, he didn't want them to acknowledge the box because that automatically insinuated there were restrictions—boundaries that shouldn't or maybe couldn't be crossed—and he wanted them to think without any hindrance at all.

British entrepreneur Theo Paphitis, another man who found *his way* to succeed with dyslexia, takes Walt Disney's idea in a slightly different direction. He acknowledges a box but understands you don't have to be burdened by it. Paphitis says, "Those with dyslexia don't just think outside the box; they build a new one" (2017). In other words, if the situation calls for a box, and there must be a box, you don't have to be captive to the existing one—the traditional, conventional, "normal," expected one. You're free to establish the dimensions that fit your solution. You name them, you set them, and you rearrange them. You don't have to make your box cubic—make it tetragonal!

Reflect on the moments when your child exhibited out-of-the-box thinking. Perhaps they found a unique solution to a problem or approached a task in an unexpected way. Appreciate their natural strengths, encourage them to explore their interests, and push them to pursue activities that allow them to demonstrate their creativity.

## How to Harness This Strength

You can help your child sharpen their creative thinking by building on these strengths and abilities.

- **Encourage creative play:** Creative play allows children to use their imagination. They can create stories, build forts, or pretend they are different characters. This type of play encourages them to explore new ideas and solutions. Facilitate creative play by providing a variety of materials, such as blocks, art supplies, or costumes, that help stimulate your child's imagination.

- **Ask open-ended questions:** These questions must be answered with more than a simple yes or no. For example, instead of asking, "Did you like the movie?" you could ask, "What did you think about the movie?" This encourages children to express their thoughts and feelings more deeply. Open-ended questions promote critical thinking and help children process information at a higher level. You can also use these questions during daily activities to encourage discussion and make deeper connections with your child.

- **Encourage exploration:** "Why?" and "How?" drive curiosity and promote a deeper understanding of concepts. Whenever a child asks these questions, it's essential to take the time to explore the answers together. If a child asks, "Why is the sky blue?" rather than giving a simple answer, you can explain how light scatters through the atmosphere to create different colours. This satisfies the child's curiosity and builds a habit of inquiry and exploration.

- **Let them colour outside the lines:** When kids are given colouring books, they might feel confined by the lines on the page. Encouraging them to colour outside those lines allows them to express their ideas without restrictions. This may involve using different colours in unexpected places or even creating their own designs. Celebrating their unique choices is important, reinforcing the concept that creativity has no right or wrong answers.

- **Allow them alone time:** Quiet time allows kids to think and process their ideas without outside influences. When children engage in solo activities, such as drawing, reading, or building, they learn to rely on their thoughts and creativity. This independence fosters self-confidence and nurtures out-of-the-box thinking. Set aside a few minutes each day for your child to enjoy their company, whether in a cozy nook or a designated play area.

- **Brainstorm with your child:** This is an excellent way to tap into your child's creativity. Make it informal and fun. Gather the family and sit down with a blank piece of paper. Present a fun problem or topic to discuss. For example, ask, "How can we make our backyard more fun?" Encourage everyone to share their ideas without judgment. Write down all suggestions. This process teaches children that all ideas are valid and valuable. They learn to build on other ideas, developing collaborative skills and a sense of community.

- **Play in nature:** Nature provides endless opportunities for exploration and creativity. Children can climb trees, gather stones, or observe insects. When they engage with the world around them, they begin to notice patterns and details they may not see indoors. Organize nature walks or outdoor activities and allow them opportunities to problem-solve. For example, see if they can lead you back home or ask them to figure out which trail to follow to reach a particular part of the park.

- **Work puzzles or problem-solving games:** Puzzles encourage children to think critically as they piece together different components. This type of play enhances their cognitive skills and promotes patience and perseverance. Parents can use various puzzle types, including jigsaw puzzles, logic puzzles, and video games that require problem-solving skills. Discussing strategies to complete the puzzles or games can further develop their analytical thinking.

- **Teach cause and effect, reasons and consequences:** This practice provides them with a foundational understanding of how their actions can influence outcomes. Simple experiments can be conducted at home, such as mixing vinegar and baking soda to observe a reaction. Through these activities, children learn to connect their actions with results. For example, when they push a toy car, they can see it move. Understanding this connection helps children make sense of the world around them and think critically about their actions.

Fostering a supportive environment is a collective responsibility involving parents, educators, peers, and the community. A culture that values creativity and diverse thinking can empower children with dyslexia to own their unique gifts and thrive. By embracing and developing out-of-the-box thinking, children with dyslexia can transition from feeling limited by their challenges to recognizing their capabilities. Through encouragement, creative activities, and real-life experiences, they can learn to navigate the world uniquely and pave the path for future success.

***

# Summary

In this chapter, we explored the strengths of thinking outside the box, highlighted the unique cognitive abilities of individuals with dyslexia, and suggested strategies to nurture these traits in academic and personal settings.

We highlighted the importance of recognizing and celebrating the strengths of dyslexic learners, offering practical techniques for educators and parents to support them. They can thrive academically and personally by focusing on what these individuals excel at rather than their struggles. This strengths-based approach nurtures innovation, adaptability, and collaboration, helping them succeed in all areas of life.

It's time for society to start accommodating and appreciating the talents and contributions of people with dyslexia instead of trying to change them or force them to abide by the traditional workings of the world.

Up next, we're diving into **MORE Strength #3: Reasoning.**

Sure, we all use our reasoning skills every day, but for the dyslexic mind, it's more than just a habit—it's a dynamic process.

Their logical, spatial, and narrative thinking doesn't just follow a straight line—it zigzags, loops, and pulls off stunts most of us wouldn't dream of. Clayton once said his thoughts were always in motion, and that's the magic of dyslexic reasoning—fluid, dynamic, and anything but predictable.

So, what does that look like in action, and how can it benefit your child both in and out of the classroom? You might discover a new way of seeing how your child's mind works.

# Chapter 5

# Strength #3 Reasoning

*It's not that I'm so smart; it's just that I stay with problems longer.*

—Albert Einstein

F or many children with dyslexia, reading and writing can feel like climbing a steep hill with no end in sight.

While pursuing my studies, I worked on a case involving a young boy named Alex, who faced significant academic challenges. Alex found school incredibly difficult. When he looked at his reading assignments, the letters often blurred together to create a jumble, and he felt defeated before he even got started. One day, during a group project to build a model of a historical landmark, something clicked for Alex.

While his classmates got tangled up in the details, he used his sharp reasoning skills to see how all the pieces could fit together. Grabbing a piece of paper, he sketched out a plan, carefully drawing where each element should go, bringing the project to life before anyone else could see it. His spatial reasoning skills kicked in and allowed him to create a virtual road map of the outcome, showing his teammates how to get from point A to point B. This moment was transformative for Alex. He realized that while reading may not be his strong suit, his ability to think logically and spatially allowed him to contribute in a way others might not.

## Dyslexic Minds Exhibit MORE Reasoning Abilities

Reasoning is a broad term involving the ability to think, understand, and form judgments. It is a fundamental skill that uses logic to make sense of the world, allowing us to draw conclusions based on information, solve problems, and make decisions. For children with dyslexia, reasoning often manifests in four main areas: logical reasoning, spatial reasoning, narrative reasoning, and dynamic reasoning. Each area is a key strength that can be recognized and nurtured in dyslexic minds.

- **Logical reasoning** revolves around analyzing situations and making decisions based on given data. It's the ability to think clearly and systematically. It involves making deductions and recognizing patterns. Strong logical reasoning skills allow children with dyslexia to process information differently, which leads them to innovative solutions that target the problem at hand. For example, while Alex struggled with reading comprehension, he excelled at solving puzzles. When you solve a puzzle, you use logical reasoning to determine which pieces fit together. This skill is essential in mathematics, where one must follow several steps to arrive at the correct answer. It is also crucial when making decisions in daily life as it allows individuals to weigh the pros and cons before arriving at a conclusion.

- **Spatial reasoning** refers to the capacity to visualize and manipulate objects in space. Children like Alex, who may struggle with written language, often have a heightened ability to understand maps and models. For instance, when playing with building blocks, they can easily envision the final structure before assembling it. To encourage this skill, you can provide opportunities for hands-on activities like puzzles, building games, and art projects that require spatial awareness. Because spatial reasoning involves understanding how different objects relate to each other in space, this skill is essential in fields such as architecture and engineering, where professionals must visualize structures before they are built. Like Alex, someone with strong spatial reasoning could look at a blueprint and quickly understand how the components fit together in the three-dimensional space. This ability is not limited to professional fields. Everyday tasks like packing a car for a trip or arranging furniture in a room also require spatial reasoning skills.

- **Narrative reasoning** is about constructing stories and understanding sequences of events. It refers to the ability to make sense of the events unfolding within yourself. Children with dyslexia often thrive in creative storytelling. They might discover that they can connect with others by sharing their ideas and stories in a way that draws people in—like telling a vivid story that sparks a conversation or explaining a complex concept with a fun, relatable example that makes everyone smile. Parents and educators can foster this skill by encouraging children to share stories verbally first, allowing them to express ideas without the writing barrier. This skill enables us to connect different pieces of information and understand the bigger picture. For instance, when reading a novel, a person uses narrative reasoning to follow the plot, understand character motivations, and grasp themes within the story. This type of reasoning is also essential in comprehending history, where understanding the sequence of events helps us learn from the past.

- **Dynamic reasoning** is the ability to apply knowledge flexibly to various situations. This involves adapting previous knowledge to new contexts and recognizing patterns. Practicing real-life problem-solving, such as cooking recipes or completing household chores, can strengthen this type of reasoning. Children can learn to make decisions based on past experiences, which will help them confidently navigate new tasks. Dynamic reasoning requires adapting your thinking based on new information or changing circumstances. Imagine playing a game where the rules can change at any moment. Players must stay alert and adjust their strategies accordingly. This skill is valuable in many professions and everyday situations as it allows individuals to remain flexible and responsive to their environment. Being able to think dynamically can enhance problem-solving abilities and facilitate effective teamwork.

By understanding how reasoning manifests, you can see how your child's unique strengths shine through in everyday activities. Observe their actions and behaviours—have you noticed any distinct ways of thinking or problem-solving? Maybe they enjoy building intricate structures with blocks to create something tall and stable, helping them visualize and understand how objects fit together in space.

These strengths can be utilized in combination. Imagine a child who struggles with traditional math problems but excels at assembling intricate puzzles. Instead of adding columns of numbers, they might picture a math problem as a set of puzzle pieces, visualizing how they fit together to find the solution. For example, when asked to calculate $3 + 4$, they don't see numbers—they see objects. They might picture three apples next to four apples and combine them into one group. This way, they're using spatial and logical reasoning to solve the problem, turning it into a mental puzzle rather than just an equation on a page.

Watch how your child tells stories. Do they provide plenty of details and engage their listeners? Children who can weave narratives with great detail often display strong verbal reasoning abilities. These kids can analyze situations and convey their thoughts coherently and captivatingly. Such dyslexic learners are like Clayton, who connects deeply with stories. They might need help writing essays, but when discussing their favourite book, they can clearly articulate the plot and character development.

Clayton exhibited this particular trait during his youth. In Chapter 1, we talked about how, though he struggled to read printed words on a page or computer screens, he understood the theme or message it presented. And when the material was presented audibly to him, he had a greater understanding than his classmates who read those exact words on a page. I noticed this with Christian as well. When I read books to him, he excitedly repeated the plot and moral with more depth and detail than the other kids in class.

Clayton shares this love for stories. He prefers listening to audiobooks but also reads written material, finding great pleasure in novels, how-tos, and inspirational works. Both boys have a knack for grasping the deeper meaning behind what's being communicated, highlighting their strength in narrative reasoning.

Acknowledging your child's reasoning abilities can serve as a source of encouragement. Positive reinforcement helps build their confidence. A simple comment like "I love how you explained that story" or "Great job figuring out how those blocks fit together" can motivate them to keep exploring these skills. Encouragement helps them feel valued and appreciated for who they are.

## *The Advantages of Reasoning Strengths*

Developing strong reasoning skills offers numerous advantages. Children with well-honed reasoning abilities often develop superior problem-solving skills. They can analyze situations, predict outcomes, and make informed decisions. This skill set is invaluable in both academic and real-world scenarios. For instance, a child who excels in reasoning may shine during group discussions, where they can connect different ideas and offer insightful conclusions.

Reasoning skills also enhance creativity. When children draw connections between ideas, they can develop innovative solutions. This enables them to think outside the box—as discussed in the last chapter—and find new ways to tackle challenges. This world is constantly changing, so having these phenomenal reasoning skills sets them apart and helps them adapt successfully.

## Practical Tools and Strategies

Understanding the strengths of reasoning in children with dyslexia is only the first step. It's crucial to provide practical tools and strategies to empower them. Parents, educators, and mentors can aid children by using effective techniques that harness this. Here are some strategies to try:

- **Encourage collaborative learning**: Group projects, like the model-building project Alex worked on, allow children with dyslexia to shine. They can rely on their peers for reading tasks while sharing their reasoning skills in planning and executing projects. Doing so promotes teamwork and builds confidence, which is invaluable in academic and social settings.

* **Integrate storytelling into learning experiences**: Whether verbally, visually, or a combination of both, storytelling can be a powerful tool. Asking children to recount a memorable event in their lives helps develop their narrative reasoning. You can create storytelling sessions at home where your child shares their tales. Ask open-ended questions that prompt them to elaborate on their ideas. Questions like "What happened next?" or "How did that make you feel?" can stimulate their imagination and help them think analytically about their stories. This practice nurtures their creativity and strengthens their ability to structure thoughts logically.

* **Celebrate small successes**: Recognizing and reinforcing their problem-solving and reasoning efforts helps build their resilience. Have them keep a journal of their accomplishments, no matter how small, and encourage them to review it periodically to see their progress over time.

* **Incorporate neighbourhood games or community projects that require reasoning**: For example, designing a community garden involves planning, measuring space, and thinking about plant placement. Engaging in activities where reasoning is put to the test allows children to apply their skills in practical, real-world scenarios.

- **Play simple strategy games**: Games like chess or checkers require players to think ahead and plan their moves. Such games encourage children to consider different scenarios and outcomes and lead to enhanced problem-solving abilities.

- **Work puzzles:** Offer puzzles or brain teasers appropriate for their age. This not only makes learning fun but also encourages them to think critically. Working through these challenges builds resilience and teaches them it's okay to struggle with a problem before finding a solution.

- **Participate in group play**: Observe how your child interacts with peers during playtime. Do they take on leadership roles and develop strategies for games? Are they good at including others and recognizing their feelings? Such social interactions often reveal critical thinking and emotional intelligence, both essential to reasoning.

- **Provide an environment that supports exploration and curiosity**: Let your child ask questions and explore topics of interest. If they show curiosity about animals, take them to a zoo or read books about wildlife together. When children feel supported in their inquiries, they're more likely to engage deeply and develop a love for learning.

- **Point out the positive**: It's crucial to emphasize the positive aspects of reasoning abilities and skills as they develop. Acknowledge their effort even when they face difficulties. Remind them that making mistakes is part of learning. When you encourage your child to embrace challenges, you instill a growth mindset that can last a lifetime.

- **Utilize activities or curricula emphasizing reasoning skills**: Explore educational games or apps focusing on logic, problem-solving, and critical thinking. Many resources are designed for different age groups, allowing children to learn through engaging and interactive experiences.

Take the time to reflect on your child's development regularly and identify the areas where they excel. Earlier, we suggested having your child keep a journal. It would also help you record their accomplishments, exciting moments, and breakthroughs so you'll notice patterns of growth in specific reasoning strengths when you look back. You and your child are in partnership on this journey. The more you understand their differences and super-skills, the better you can tailor activities to their strengths and support their growth along those paths.

Don't hesitate to share your observations with teachers or other caregivers; they should also be encouraged to provide you with additional insights and strategies to support your child's reasoning development.

Remember to be patient as you support your child in recognizing and developing their strengths. Each child's journey is unique. Your role is to encourage exploration and engagement in a way that resonates with their interests and fosters an environment where their unique talents can shine.

## Reasoning in the Real World

Richard Branson struggled with dyslexia throughout his school years. However, he found ways to excel by focusing on his strengths. He often mentions how his reasoning skills helped him develop innovative ideas and make strategic business decisions. Rather than being held back by difficulties in reading, he used his unique way of thinking to create a global brand.

Another inspiring example is actor and producer Whoopi Goldberg. Goldberg struggled with dyslexia as a child, but she did not let it define her. Instead, she honed her reasoning skills and embraced her creativity. She often speaks about how her ability to think differently helped her succeed in the entertainment industry. By sharing her story, she inspires countless children with dyslexia to embrace their reasoning strengths and pursue their dreams.

These stories highlight the importance of children with dyslexia and those who support them in focusing on strengths instead of limitations. Imagine possibilities and overlook barriers. Reassure your child, build them up, and point out even their smallest victories to boost their confidence and courage and help them feel capable and willing to take on new challenges. Create an environment where they can see that their unique abilities are not just different but powerful tools for success, even if their journey doesn't match their peers.

## How to Harness This Strength

Teach your child how to harness this strength. Kids Pediatrics suggests the following exercises by age to help your child build these skills (FOKP, 2021):

- **Birth–age 2**

  - Encourage imagination and pretend play.

  - Encourage curiosity.

  - Provide creative toys.

  - Experiment with hands-on games and toys.

  - Help them put words to their emotions and feelings.

- **Ages 3–5**

  - Encourage them to explore their world and the things in it.

  - Teach them to manage their feelings.

  - Invite questions.

  - Allow free play.

  - Ask open-ended questions.

- Let them learn by trial and error (safely).

- Encourage them to predict outcomes.

- Help them make connections within patterns.

- **Ages 6–9**

  - Encourage reading.

  - Allow them to experience failure; don't just bail them out.

  - Accept their mistakes and teach them to do so as well.

  - Don't overschedule activities.

  - Allow your child to have downtime.

  - Encourage them to solve problems; don't jump in and give them solutions.

  - Ask questions to make them think.

  - Let them develop their own opinions.

  - Allow them to arrive at their own conclusions, but gently correct them if necessary.

  - Assess their decisions without casting judgment.

  - Provide a safe environment for them to decompress and release intense feelings.

- **Ages 10 and up**

  - Model critical thinking for them in your own life.

  - Limit their screen time on devices, TV, and gaming.

  - Provide resources for learning and growth, like internet access, encyclopedias, or a library card.

  - Encourage them to stretch their wings and develop independence.

  - Ask for their opinion and discuss how they arrived at that decision.

  - Don't just fix your kids' mistakes; guide them through them and help them to learn from their experiences.

  - Give your kids guidance on creating their own schedules and choosing their own activities, and help them adhere to family regulations.

Reasoning allows us to analyze information, think critically, and make informed decisions. Next, we'll look at various techniques you can use to help your child harness and develop this skill as they grow toward improved problem-solving abilities and better decision-making skills:

- **Ask questions that prompt more questions**: Instead of simply providing answers or explanations, ask children questions that spur them to think deeper. For example, if a child says they believe dogs are better than cats, you might ask, "What makes you feel that way?" or, "How do you think other people might feel about that?" These types of questions foster a curiosity that encourages children to not only express their thoughts but also consider the views of others. This method can help them develop the habit of questioning their own assumptions.

- **Introduce multiple perspectives**: Help children learn to appreciate that there are various sides to an issue. For instance, when discussing the environment, present viewpoints from different stakeholders like environmentalists, local businesses, or government officials. By exposing children to a range of opinions, they can better understand the complexities of specific issues. Encourage them to consider how each perspective could lead to different conclusions or solutions, helping to cultivate open-mindedness and critical thinking—two essential elements of effective reasoning.

- **Encourage decision-making**: Give children opportunities to make their own decisions. When they face choices, encourage them to think through the possible outcomes. For example, if a child decides what game to play with friends, ask them to consider everyone's preferences and how each choice might affect the group's mood. You can guide them by asking questions like "What do your friends enjoy doing?" or "How do you think each option will make everyone feel?" Empowering children to make decisions fosters independence and teaches them to think critically about the implications of their choices.

- **Connect dissimilar information:** Help children connect dissimilar pieces of information to analyze the overall situation better. For example, when discussing a topic like health, you might bring in nutrition, exercise, and mental well-being. Encourage children to think about how these areas influence each other by asking questions like "How does what we eat affect how we feel?" or "In what ways can exercise improve our mood?" This will help them see the bigger picture and improve their analytical skills. By developing the ability to connect different areas of knowledge, children can form well-rounded understandings of complex subjects.

- **Teach problem-solving skills**: Teaching children how to work toward solutions is essential for developing strong reasoning skills. Present them with challenges or problems to solve, but guide them to take the lead in finding solutions. For instance, if there's a conflict among friends, encourage the children to brainstorm possible resolutions. Ask questions like "What are some ways we can solve this?" and "What would happen if we try this approach?" This practice helps them find an approach and teaches them the importance of collaboration and communication.

- **Engage the local community**: Take learning outside the classroom to enhance children's reasoning abilities. Organizing a local community walk can provide them with real-world experiences that stimulate their thinking. As they learn about their surroundings, encourage them to ask questions about the area's history, the people who live there, and the environment. You could ask, "What do you notice about the buildings?" or, "Why do you think this area is important to the community?" Engage them in discussions about local issues, such as sustainability or community safety, to provide practical applications for their reasoning skills.

Asking children these questions guides them to consider multiple perspectives, make their own decisions, connect different pieces of information, problem-solve, and engage with their community. It also creates a rich environment in which reasoning can thrive.

***

# Summary

Children with dyslexia have MORE reasoning skills. We saw this in Alex, a boy who struggled with reading but demonstrated strong spatial reasoning during a group project. Later in the chapter, we explored three other areas of reasoning—logical, narrative, and dynamic—and stressed the importance of identifying and nurturing these skills. We also offered practical strategies, such as using visual aids, encouraging collaborative learning, integrating storytelling, and celebrating small successes to support the development of children with dyslexia. While reading may be difficult for dyslexic learners, their exceptional deduction skills can lead to success in various aspects of life, from school to work and beyond.

The next chapter will examine **MORE Strength #4: Expression.** We'll explore the vibrant world of creativity and imagination, revealing one of the most remarkable dyslexic strengths—one that brings ideas to life in unexpected ways. But what does it really mean to express ourselves, and how often do we stop to think about the power behind it in our daily lives?

# Chapter 6

# Strength #4 Expression

*Your brain is much better than you think; just use it!*
—Leonardo Da Vinci

R emarkable creativity and powerful imagination com-
pose the fourth and final MORE strength of dyslexic
minds: expression.

In elementary school, John "was, like many children with
dyslexia in education, remarkably intelligent yet severely
undervalued" (*Was John Lennon Dyslexic?*, 2020). Although
he found stories delightful and enjoyed making up tales
of his own, John had great difficulty spelling. And while he
drafted clever poems and recited them orally, he could not
remember the verses other people had written. In fact, John
often listened to the music of Elvis Presley and Chuck Berry
growing up, but because he couldn't recall their lyrics, he
invented new words to fit their melodies.

John excelled in art classes, but his other school grades were rock-bottom, and he dropped out before completing his education. However, the school director, recognizing John's profound intellect—despite his poor grades—and firmly believing he would "flourish in the creative sector," recommended him to an arts college.

John was particularly gifted at singing, composing music by ear, and playing the guitar. Despite his Aunt Mimi's discouragement, saying, "The guitar is all very well, John, but you will never make a living out of it," the determined teen formed his own band.

Because reading and writing have been integral skills to master in academics for so long, instructors have wrongly identified people with dyslexia as less intelligent, ignorant, or careless. That attitude turned young John Lennon away from formal education and onto the world stage.

John wondered about that implication as well, later stating,

People like me know they are so-called geniuses at ten, eight, nine... I always wondered, "Why has nobody discovered me?" No one recognized that I was more clever than the others at school. Did they even realize how clueless the teachers were? All they offered was information I didn't need. (Lennon, n.d.)

Kids like young John Lennon often find ways to express their feelings through art or storytelling. Creative outlets can give them relief and joy, allowing them to channel their thoughts into something tangible. Parents and educators must recognize these outlets and encourage children to create.

As you read about the strength of expression, consider moments when your child has showcased this trait. Perhaps they told a captivating story, created a beautiful piece of art, or empathized with a friend in distress. Reflect on these moments and encourage your child to express themself so they can discover a sense of pride and hope and develop greater confidence and joy in their abilities.

## Empowering Children With Dyslexia

Empowering children with dyslexia requires nurturing their imaginative capabilities. Imagination is not just about daydreaming; it's about thinking beyond the ordinary. This heightened sensitivity to the world around them can foster creativity. Parents can engage their children in storytelling games when encouraging imaginative play. For instance, one might start with, "Once upon a time, there was a little dragon who couldn't breathe fire," and the child can add, "But instead, it could make flowers bloom with a single breath." This way, you build a story together, letting your child's imagination take the lead and helping them develop critical thinking, problem-solving, and communication abilities.

In the classroom setting, teachers can create an environment that invites expression. This could mean incorporating more visual aids in lessons. For example, instead of reading a chapter from a textbook, a teacher might present a video or slideshow emphasizing imagery. This strategy helps children like young John Lennon better understand the material, brings the learning experience to life, and makes it engaging and memorable.

## *Practical Strategies for Support*

To nourish these strengths, you can employ several strategies:

- **Maintain open communication:** Create safe spaces where your child feels comfortable sharing their thoughts. This could mean dedicating time each week for family discussions where everyone gets a chance to speak without interruption.

- **Introduce art projects that encourage expression**: Painting, sculpting, or writing stories can be relaxing and promote a sense of accomplishment.

- **Read them stories about other children with dyslexia:** This will help your child feel like they're not alone and demonstrate how other kids might overcome the challenges dyslexia puts in their path.

- **Partner with your child's teachers to build a support network:** You could collaborate on strategies that help your child navigate learning challenges, like developing personalized learning plans with goals tailored to your child's strengths. They could focus on visual learning techniques or project-based assessments that allow for varied modes of expression.

- **Recognize your child's progress**: This will motivate them to continue pursuing these gifts. If your child finishes a drawing or short story, display it proudly at home to boost their self-esteem. It validates their

uniqueness and shows them you value all their trea-
sured talents. Your encouraging words, as can those
of friends, family, and teachers, can go a long way.

# Dyslexic Minds Show MORE Expression

Expression is the ability to convey thoughts, feelings, and
ideas clearly and creatively. It encompasses a variety of skills
and abilities that allow individuals to communicate effectively and genuinely with others:

- **Imaginative expression** involves thinking outside
  the box and generating new ideas or perspectives.
  Children who come up with unique stories or solutions to problems use their creativity to *engage* others.

- **Creative expression** is the way people use artistic mediums such as painting, writing, or music to
  share their inner thoughts and emotions. Imagine a
  child painting a bright, sunlit sky with splashes of
  yellow and orange, their brushstrokes full of energy
  and movement. On another day, they might paint
  a cloudy, deep blue sea with darker shades, their
  strokes slower and more deliberate. Through these
  colours and shapes, they're telling a story—one that
  captures feelings of joy or sadness that words alone
  might not express. Creative expression allows individuals to explore their identities and communicate
  their experiences in a way that can *resonate* with others.

- **Empathy** is seeing the world through someone else's lens, catching the subtle details that might otherwise go unnoticed, and understanding their feelings from a fresh perspective. Imagine a child noticing a classmate struggling to read aloud during a lesson. Remembering their own difficulties with reading, the child quietly leans over, gives a reassuring smile, and whispers, "You're doing great. I used to find that tricky, too." Children with dyslexia often develop strong empathy skills because their personal experiences can make them more sensitive to the feelings of others.

Empathy is essential for building strong relationships and nurturing a supportive environment, whether at home, in school, or with friends. This ability can help children forge deeper connections with their peers. It's *especially* important for children with dyslexia because understanding and relating to others makes them feel less isolated, helping them build friendships based on trust, kindness, and mutual support.

Encourage discussions about emotions and experiences at home to enhance these skills further. A simple activity could involve sharing stories in small groups about times when they felt misunderstood or frustrated. Role-playing scenarios where children practice understanding one another's feelings can also be particularly effective, like acting out a situation in which one child feels sad and another offers support. By taking on these roles, children with dyslexia can learn valuable social skills while feeling understood, reinforcing that they are not alone in their challenges.

I'm sure you did already, but the bonus bundle also offers more resources on how to encourage creative expression. Scan the QR in case you haven't downloaded it yet.

To further illustrate the strength of expression, let's say your child has been assigned to work on a group project at school. Your child—who demonstrates imaginative expression—might suggest an idea no one else thought of, and it could inspire the entire group. This kind of innovation can lead to a more engaging and successful project.

Creative expression can shine during a group project when your child contributes by designing a poster with their own drawings and suggests that the group present their ideas visually. Empathy plays a role in this process as children listen to each other's ideas and feelings, ensuring everyone feels included and valued.

These examples highlight how expression is not just about communicating but also about connecting with people. A child who expresses themself well can encourage their peers to do the same. It creates a positive cycle of communication in which everyone's voice is heard. This not only benefits a child with dyslexia's social skills but also enhances their emotional intelligence and makes them more adaptable as they navigate different environments.

## Expression in the Real World

When volunteering at a school in Toronto, I met a 10-year-old girl named Sophie, who has dyslexia. One day in class, she was trying to explain her idea for a project to her classmates. She had a clear picture in her mind, but as soon as she started to speak, the words got tangled, and she couldn't find the right way to express herself. I could see her frustration building, but instead of giving up, Sophie grabbed a marker, walked up to the board, and began sketching her idea. She showed the class exactly what she meant in just a few quick strokes, and everyone understood. It was a moment of pure clarity—Sophie's dyslexia didn't hold her back; it simply made her find another way to communicate. Aside from reading and writing abilities, dyslexia also impacts how children communicate their thoughts and feelings.

When children learn to use adaptive ways to express themselves clearly, they overcome many dyslexia-related challenges. Finding new methods to communicate their thoughts builds confidence and helps them connect with others meaningfully.

When children cultivate their expression skills, they can share ideas and opinions more effectively, as Sophie did. This opens the door to teamwork. Children can bring their unique perspectives and collaborate effectively by clearly expressing their ideas during group projects or discussions.

Expression skills make a difference. Recall television personality Jay Leno's story from Chapter 3. When he became a late-night talk show host, he had trouble reading the written words on the teleprompters, so he made up his own discourse as he went along. Because he has MORE strengths, he could display improvisational ingenuity and *express* his points passionately and persuasively when speaking. This ability helped him perform well in that situation and boosted his confidence.

Your child's strong command of expression will lead to greater participation in class discussions and a willingness to participate in extracurricular activities. It will also give them the confidence to stand up for themselves, dissuade negative comments, and bust those myths we discussed in Chapter 1. More importantly, it will provide them with a voice to help classmates, teachers, and employers understand how dyslexia is a learning difference, not a disability, not a hindrance, and not something that makes them less than others.

## *Success Stories of Dyslexic Individuals and Their Expression Skills*

Many well-known individuals with dyslexia have significantly contributed to the arts and creative industries, turning their uniqueness into something remarkable. This doesn't mean your child will become a celebrity or business magnate—although they certainly could—but it highlights that while dyslexia may complicate traditional learning methods, it also opens doors to other equally valuable and impactful forms of expression.

Actress Whoopi Goldberg has publicly shared her struggles with dyslexia and how it made school difficult for her. Whoopi's ability to express herself through characters has made her a successful actress and a powerful advocate for those with learning differences.

Richard Branson, founder of the Virgin Group—which includes the Virgin Records music label, Virgin Atlantic airlines, Virgin Rail Group train travel, and Virgin Galactic spaceflight—struggled with dyslexia during his school years. He often found it challenging to keep up academically. However, he discovered he had a talent for entrepreneurship. Branson has used his expression skills to share his vision and connect with others in the business. His journey shows that skills of expression can turn challenges into stepping stones to success.

The experiences of people like Whoopi Goldberg and Richard Branson teach us that developing expression skills can lead to personal and professional growth. One key lesson is the value of practice. Just as learning to read takes time, becoming proficient in expressing oneself requires effort. Encouraging children to practice speaking, storytelling, and even drawing their ideas can strengthen their confidence in sharing thoughts.

It's essential to recognize that everyone has unique strengths. Just because a child struggles with reading does not mean they lack talent elsewhere. Fostering expression skills can provide them with the means to navigate life's challenges effectively. Children with dyslexia can thrive when given opportunities to validate their voices and share their talents.

## Inspiring the Next Generation

Children with dyslexia bring fresh perspectives to the table; their brains are wired to see patterns, solve problems, and connect ideas in ways others might overlook. This dynamic thinking can lead to breakthroughs in art, technology, design, and social change. Allowing children to express themselves can fundamentally change how society perceives learning differences, inspire new ways to adapt to them, and redefine the standards of success.

By nurturing this open mindset, we can create environments where children with dyslexia feel empowered to explore and express their talents. Community programs can also serve as excellent resources for children with dyslexia. Workshops focused on public speaking, drama, and communication can enhance expression skills while providing a space for interaction with peers dealing with similar challenges. These activities not only develop skills but also build friendships and support networks that are essential for emotional growth.

Role models play a significant part in this development. When children see successful individuals who have overcome similar challenges, they can draw inspiration from their journeys. Workshops and mentorship programs involving adults with dyslexia who have thrived in their careers can motivate young dyslexic learners and reinforce the idea that they can excel and achieve their dreams with determination and support.

## How to Harness This Strength

To harness and further develop expression, adopt techniques and strategies that promote creativity and empathy.

### *Creativity*

To unlock your child's creativity, consider the following techniques:

- **Show examples that spark ideas**: For instance, looking at various art styles can inspire someone to try different techniques in their own work. If your child enjoys painting, they might explore abstract, realism, or impressionist styles to see what resonates with them.

- **Encourage experimentation:** This could mean letting your child set up a pretend restaurant at home, where they create a menu, take orders, and "serve" meals using their toys or snacks from the kitchen. They can make up dishes, set the table, and decide on the restaurant's name and theme. The goal isn't about getting everything right but enjoying the fun of role-playing and improvising. This playful activity encourages creativity and problem-solving and helps them express their ideas without the pressure of perfection.

- **Provide a wide variety of materials**: Providing a variety of cooking ingredients and kitchen tools can also inspire creativity in a child's daily routine. For example, a child might start by helping make simple sandwiches but then discover a love for experimenting with different flavours and textures, like adding new toppings or creating fun shapes. They may enjoy mixing ingredients, testing out recipes, and even making up their own snacks. By giving them access to different foods and utensils, they can explore, play, and learn, all while developing a sense of independence and creative problem-solving.

- **Embrace various art forms:** This means valuing not just traditional art forms but also crafts, cooking, writing, and even building. Each of these activities allows for expressiveness in different ways. For example, building with LEGO or other construction sets can be a creative outlet where your child imagines and designs their own structures. Recognizing various ways to make things can build confidence and encourage exploration in diverse fields.

- **Emphasize the process and not just the product**: Focusing on *how* your child creates can lead to a more enjoyable and fulfilling experience. For example, writing poetry in a journal—or reciting poems into a recording file on their electronic device—can be an act of self-reflection in which the words are not meant for anyone else to see or hear. The act of writing alone can be therapeutic and enlightening. Celebrating the journey of creation can motivate individuals to express themselves without fearing judgment.

## *Empathy*

Follow these suggestions to help develop empathy in your child and help them cultivate effective expression:

- **Demonstrate understanding and support**: Picture your child retreating to their room after a rough day, shoulders tense, and eyes downcast. Instead of giving advice, you knock gently, sit beside them, and say, "Tell me about what happened today." As they start to share, you're fully there, just listening, no fixes, no interruptions—just quiet understanding. Sometimes, all they need is to feel heard, and in that moment, you're teaching them the power of empathy. You'd be amazed at how far active listening can go in making them feel safe and genuinely valued.

- **Discuss emotions:** Engage in simple conversations

about how various situations make your child feel. This approach helps them understand that emotions are valid and worth discussing, which, in turn, nurtures their ability to empathize with others.

- **Celebrate empathetic behaviour**: Acknowledge and celebrate moments when your child shows kindness or empathy. For example, if they comfort a friend who's feeling down, highlight how meaningful their actions are and encourage them to keep being supportive. This kind of positive feedback strengthens these behaviours.

- **Incorporate elements of creativity and empathy into expression**: By using examples, encouraging exploration, providing resources, emphasizing processes, and modelling kindness, you can create a nurturing environment that promotes a culture of openness and creativity and allows your child to express themself freely.

- **Use various tools and approaches:** Creativity and empathy are intertwined. Keep the emphasis on exploration and understanding—whether expressed through art, writing, or conversations—and help your child achieve richer self-expression and stronger relationships with others.

Nurturing your child's talent for expression can help them thrive in personal relationships and social settings. While challenges might arise, their expressive capabilities can shine brightly as they find new and more efficient ways to communicate. By encouraging them to express their feelings and set clear boundaries, you support their growth in emotional maturity and understanding of how to treat others—and how *they* deserve to be treated.

***

## Summary

In this chapter, we explored the **MORE Strength #4: Expression.** Children with dyslexia often possess extraordinary imagination and creativity, which can become powerful assets. Think of young John Lennon, who, despite his intelligence, struggled in school and left before finishing. He found his MORE superpower in expression, channeling his emotions through music and lyrics.

By encouraging creative outlets, you can help your child build confidence and self-esteem. Parents can nurture their children's imaginative abilities to boost critical thinking and communication, while teachers can foster expressive classrooms with visuals to support understanding.

Developing expression skills empowers children with dyslexia to articulate their thoughts despite reading and writing challenges. Stories like Richard Branson's illustrate how skills like creativity and empathy can pave the way to success. Fostering these qualities helps build a supportive environment that encourages connection and emotional growth.

As we move ahead, we'll begin the third and final section of this book: **The World of Opportunities for Dyslexic Brilliance.** We'll discuss the impact of various parenting styles as we uncover ways you can help your child thrive at home, school, and social situations.  We'll also uncover ways the world can begin to embrace how much MORE dyslexic minds have to offer instead of skewing dyslexia to fit the world's demands.

# Part 3: The World of Opportunities for Dyslexic Brilliance

# Chapter 7

# Making the World a Better Place for Dyslexic Learners

*Dyslexia is a different brain organization that needs different teaching methods. It is never the child's fault, but rather the responsibility of us who teach to find strategies that work for that child.*

—Dr. Maryanne Wolf

P arenting is a journey filled with ups and downs, laughter and tears. For parents of children with dyslexia, this journey can often feel even more challenging. When Clayton was in elementary school, his mom, Vicki, often sat at the dining room table watching her son struggle with his reading homework. Despite her encouragement, Clayton couldn't sense the letters on the page, and she wished she could somehow do it for him. The frustration was palpable for both mother and son, and Vicki frequently felt helpless. This moment is an everyday reality for many parents of children with dyslexia, and if it describes you, you need to know you're not alone.

Acknowledging these experiences validates your feelings as you help your child navigate this complex world where traditional learning methods may not always work.

As a parent, the home is your domain. You guide and guard your child in other areas, but the family unit is the basis of your child's experiences. It needs to be a place where they feel entirely safe to be themselves—free from judgment, mockery or harsh words, and where love flows unconditionally. Imagine what it could mean for them and you to have that foundation of trust and acceptance within your family.

You can nurture this sense of security in your child by creating a foundation that helps them thrive—not in spite of their dyslexia, nor solely because of it, but by embracing it as part of who they are. Supporting them in this way equips them to succeed with their dyslexia, walking through life hand in hand with it.

You can't overcome dyslexia, but you can help manage its effects—and that's where your focus should start.

When your child attends school, you don't just turn your kid over to the administration and hope for the best. As we've seen with Clayton's and Christian's experiences, school personnel in any economic or cultural setting can be equally untrained and unequipped to properly manage, educate, and instruct children with dyslexic tendencies. Your child depends on you, their parent, to advocate for them by understanding available resources and accommodations and ensuring their academic system is informed with the most current and effective teaching methods. This sometimes includes setting up an individualized education program (IEP) or 504 plan to support your child's learning needs and provide them with accommodations, such as extended test times, access to audiobooks, or speech-to-text technology. Maintaining open communication with your child's teachers is the key to success here.

Social environments can be harsh for children with dyslexia. They may struggle with communication or social inclusion. This may be due to either ostracism from kids at school who view dyslexia as something to be mocked or to the child's own insecurities about their perceived differences. Discuss dyslexia openly with your child to help them understand it and empower them to advocate for themself. Help them build self-esteem and develop resilience. Please encourage them to participate in activities they excel at and celebrate small successes to reinforce a positive self-image.

## At Home With Dyslexia

Let's simplify parenting to some basics before we discuss how to make the home a better place for your child.

Four basic parenting styles apply across the board. They describe you and your methods and are not dependent on your child's abilities or tendencies. You must identify and understand your unique parenting style because it can significantly influence your child's emotional and academic growth.

Each of the four main types of parenting styles has unique traits that impact how children learn and thrive (Cardine, 2023b):

- **Authoritarian:** Authoritarian parents typically set strict rules and expect obedience. These parents want their kids to follow the rules without exception—and sometimes, these rules are not explained or clearly defined. For parents of children with dyslexia, this approach may lead to increased feelings of inadequacy and stress because following the rules is not cut-and-dried for them. Instead of fostering a love for learning, this style can create an environment in which a child feels afraid to speak up, fearing punishment for mistakes. This fear can intensify the struggles children with dyslexia already face with reading and writing.

- **Authoritative:** Authoritative parenting, on the other hand, combines high expectations with warmth and support. Authoritative parents explain the reasons behind rules and encourage open communication. This style can be beneficial for a child who struggles with dyslexia. These children often thrive in an environment where they feel understood and supported. They receive guidance without feeling overwhelmed, which allows them to build confidence in their abilities.

- **Permissive or indulgent:** Permissive parents are more lenient and often avoid imposing rules or following up with consequences. While this approach may seem compassionate because it is nonjudgmental and sets a low bar of expectation, it can leave children with dyslexia without the structure they need. Some may struggle to develop vital skills as clear boundaries and expectations aren't consistently enforced. This lack of direction can hinder academic progress and the development of a routine to help them progress.

- **Uninvolved or neglectful:** Uninvolved parenting is characterized by a lack of responsiveness to a child's needs. These parents don't set many rules and leave the child to lead themself. They may be physically present, loving, and kind, but their parenting leaves much to be desired. This style can leave children, especially those with dyslexia, feeling ignored and unsupported. Without adequate guidance and encouragement, these children might not receive the necessary resources to overcome their challenges. They might struggle in school and struggle to form emotional connections with their parents.

## The Best Parenting Style for Dyslexic Children

After examining these styles, the authoritative approach is often the most effective for children, especially those with dyslexia, because it emphasizes understanding, support, and structure. It allows parents to set expectations while providing the emotional backing children need. Parents can encourage their children to seek help without fear of judgment while promoting resilience and independence. Counsellor and author Thad Cardine describes the pros of author-itative parenting (2023b):

Children of authoritative parents can self-regulate. They're confident and responsible, and they manage emotions well. They bond well with their parents, feel satisfied in their family relationships, have high self-esteem, and do well in school (p. 16–17). These are ideal circumstances for any child, dyslexic or not.

### *Reflecting on Your Parenting Style*

Understanding your parenting style can be valuable for sup-porting your child with dyslexia. To assist with this, consider the following worksheet. Ask yourself these questions:

- How do I respond when my child struggles with homework?

_____

_____

_____

- Do I set clear expectations for my child's learning?

_____

_____

_____

- Am I open to discussing challenges with my child?

_____

_____

_____

- How do I show support for my child's homework ef-forts?

_____

_____

_____

- What changes can I make to become a more support-ive parent?

_____

_____

_____

Take your time to reflect on these questions. They can help you gain insights into your parenting approach and identify areas for improvement.

## Adapting Your Parenting Style

Changing or improving your parenting style might seem daunting, but small steps can lead to significant changes. Start by communicating openly with your child. Create an environment in which they feel safe expressing their frustrations. Listen to their feelings and assure them it's okay to have difficulties. Emphasize the importance of effort over perfection. Encourage them to try even when they fail.

You can also adapt your style by implementing routines that cater to their unique needs. For example, consider setting aside specific times for reading each day. Use tools that aid their learning, such as audiobooks, coloured lenses, or specialized apps designed for dyslexic learners. You might also consider exploring the possibility of working with tutors who specialize in teaching children with dyslexia.

### *Create a Welcoming Home Environment*

An understanding and compassionate home can create the ideal backdrop for a child with dyslexia. Consider these suggestions:

- **Create a designated, distraction-free space for studying:** Keep it organized and equipped with the necessary tools, such as books, writing materials, and tech devices that support their learning. This space should feel inviting and comforting.

- **Establish a routine that balances study and relaxation.** This approach helps your child feel secure and know what to expect on a daily basis. Acknowledge their efforts with praise or rewards, no matter how minor they may appear. This positive reinforcement can motivate them to continue progressing in their learning journey.

- **Utilize multisensory teaching methods:** Hands-on activities like writing letters in sand or using colourful letter blocks can enhance learning and make it appealing and enjoyable. It's okay to get messy.

- **Involve your child in selecting their study materials and supplies:** This can increase their sense of ownership over their learning process. Please encourage them to express what works best for them and not others. Building a space that resonates with their needs sends a powerful message that their learning style is valid and valued.

Creating a supportive home environment with the appropriate parenting style is a solid first step. When Clayton was first diagnosed with dyslexia, Tom, his father, worried about how this would impact Clayton's education and self-esteem. Tom remembered his own school days and how kids often picked on those they saw as different or needed extra help, and he wanted to avoid that for his son. The thought of his son being bullied pushed Tom into a state of denial—he convinced himself there was nothing wrong with his boy, hoping he could avoid the label altogether and what it implied. He continued with "regular" vocabulary and spelling drills, went through math fact flashcards, and used traditional learning methods with Clayton for quite some time. Watching Clayton's frustration as he struggled with basic reading and writing concepts broke Tom's heart. He finally faced the reality that dyslexia wasn't something he could push through with conventional methods—it needed understanding, not resistance.

After attending workshops, meeting with experts, and educating himself about learning differences, Tom began to see Clayton's *dis*abilities for what they truly were: super*abilities*. Once Tom and Vicki realized dyslexia didn't reflect Clayton's intelligence but was just a different way of processing information, they adapted their parenting style to create a supportive environment at home and be better advocates for Clayton at school.

Tom and Vicki established a structured home learning environment with a dedicated evening study time, where they both worked with Clayton on various subjects and assignments. They also established a daily reading routine, selecting books with relatable characters and storylines that captivated Clayton. They often read together, encouraging him to act out scenes and share his unique interpretations, fostering his confidence and communication skills.

With a supportive family and home atmosphere, Clayton's academic performance improved. He was more engaged in school and collaborated with his teachers. Tom and Vicki significantly enhanced Clayton's academic, emotional, and personal development by adapting their parenting styles. They showed that with support and understanding, parents can help children overcome the challenges dyslexia presents and reach their full potential.

Craft an environment that nurtures your child's growth and confidence. With the proper support, your child *can* thrive and embrace the learning journey ahead.

# At School With Dyslexia

At the start of each new school year, classrooms fill with eager faces of students who have bright hopes and dreams for their futures. However, for children with dyslexia and other learning needs, that excitement is overshadowed by the struggle to read and write. These kids are often over- whelmed by the demands of school, where learning some- times seems like climbing a mountain whose peak tran- scends the clouds.

As a parent, you've likely watched with concern as your child faced challenges like decoding words during reading lessons or getting frustrated with written assignments. Though they may not always express it compassionately, your child's teachers may also feel helpless when they can't find ways to support them effectively. These experiences resonate deeply for all involved, and parents, teachers, and kids can each feel the weight of these challenges. However, a com- mon thread of hope endures with cooperation, dedication, and perseverance.

Creating a dyslexia-friendly classroom is essential to help- ing these students thrive because an environment that em- braces their unique learning needs encourages students to harness their strengths and interests. Such a classroom em- phasizes a supportive approach to learning while maintain- ing high expectations. Instead of relying solely on timed tests or heavy text materials, teachers can offer various alterna- tives for students to show what they know. This might in- clude using project-based assessments, oral presentations, or creative assignments that allow creativity and understanding without the added stress of traditional formats. The goal is to create an atmosphere in which students with dyslexia can engage deeply with the material without feeling overwhelmed.

To foster this understanding effectively, teachers can implement specific teaching strategies tailored to their needs:

- **Multisensory learning:** This approach combines visual, auditory, and kinesthetic elements to help reinforce learning through various channels. For example, when teaching phonics, a teacher might use letter tiles for students to manipulate physically, say the sounds aloud, and visualize the letters written on a board. This engages multiple senses, making it easier for dyslexic learners to grasp the concepts. As a very young boy, Clayton benefited tremendously by being allowed to experiment with hands-on manipulatives, walk or move around the room as he processed information, and express himself in unconventional ways. Likewise, Christian thrived when he could express his understanding of stories by creating artistic representations in murals. During my limited time in Venezuela, I read aloud to Christian, engaged him in multisensory activities, and helped him connect phonetics to letters by having him trace individual letters on sandpaper while saying them out loud. I suggested his teacher give him extra time for assignments, front-row seating to minimize distraction, and visual aids for class. I also shared interactive reading and hands-on activities with my psychologist colleagues to support his learning outside class.

- **Assistive technology:** Devices or applications designed to support learning can significantly help students with dyslexia. For example, text-to-speech software allows students to hear text read aloud, making it easier to comprehend and engage with reading materials. Similarly, digital note-taking tools can help organize thoughts without the need to write everything down, which can be a barrier for many students.

- **The Orton-Gillingham approach:** This multisensory, systematic, and sequential technique focuses on clear and structured instruction. Teachers trained in this method provide individualized lessons that cater specifically to the learning profiles of their dyslexic students by meeting them at their level, pacing the introduction of new material according to the student's capabilities, and using positive reinforcement to encourage their progress.

- **Classroom accommodations:** Individualized education programs (IEPs) are tailored educational plans outlining specific learning goals and any accommodations needed for an individual student. The IEP process involves assessing the child's needs, setting measurable goals, and regularly reviewing progress. Setting goals within the IEP requires clear communication between parents and educators to ensure the goals are realistic and achievable.

- **504 plans:** If a student has disabilities but does not

require an IEP, they may utilize accommodations like preferential seating and extended test time provided by a 504 plan. A 504 plan can allow for adjustments in the learning environment and teaching methods. Parents can apply for one by submitting relevant documentation and collaborating with school staff to outline the specific accommodations the child may need to succeed.

When you approach your child's school staff about accommodations, gather and present documentation outlining your child's needs and challenges. Be sure that all relevant school officials, including teachers and special education staff, are involved in discussing the child's needs. Clearly articulate the required accommodations and draft an IEP or 504 plan collaboratively. Follow up regularly to be sure the agreed-upon plan is being executed effectively and to see if any adjustments need to be made.

Remind school personnel that dyslexia is not a mental or cognitive malfunction and does not indicate a child's level of intelligence or limit their learning potential.

Highlight your child's MORE strengths to their educators. Show them that what may seem like hindrances are unique abilities. These can bring fresh insights and potential for innovation to your child's learning experience—and to the classroom as a whole. Through conscious efforts of school systems, supportive strategies, and advocacy, students with dyslexia will progress. It's all about providing an environment in which learning is accessible, enjoyable, and encouraging.

# In Social Settings With Dyslexia

A child with dyslexia stares down at the page, letters swirling and shifting like a puzzle with no solution. They grip their pencil tighter, hands a bit shaky, feeling the weight of the classroom around them. It's not just the hard words—it's the dread of falling behind, the sinking feeling of being different. Glancing around, they see friends moving easily through their work while they're trapped in a silent struggle, a knot of frustration and loneliness tightening in their chest. It's a feeling beyond the classroom, a quiet ache of wanting someone to understand.

The thing is, they don't want to feel different. They want to fit in. They know they need extra help with certain aspects but don't want to be singled out. They don't want to be seen in the "special" classes or being tutored after school.

Barbara Pearce, a mother of two adult children with dyslexia, speaks of how her kids struggled with various aspects of their education growing up but weren't diagnosed until later in life (n.d.). Because their overall progress was in line with or above grade level, their difficulties didn't stand out and were not addressed until both kids were in their teens. When their son was diagnosed with dyslexia, he admitted he had spent years working extra hard just to avoid being labelled. For that sake, he also refused to accept accommodations in college. Instead, he developed strong relationships and bonds with his professors and administrators, which helped him navigate any academic difficulties.

A Reddit user, WeCanAllWin, shared a similar story about the fear of being known as *different* during their adolescence (2019). They were diagnosed with dyslexia, dyscalculia, and ADD when they were in about the second or third grade, and they hated school. They were embarrassed for being pulled out of classes to be tested, having a specialized tutor sit at a desk beside them in class, and being taken to special learning rooms. They felt "worthless seeing all the students and my friends around me succeed, and I can't even complete a simple task without help." The Reddit user says the experience led to them having horrible anxiety in high school over the fear of being labelled. When their so-called friends mocked them with words like "slow," "retarded," or "special," they acted unfazed. In reality, it hurt deeply enough that, at least once, they slipped away to the restroom to cry in secret. The fear lingered into adulthood; after facing one job rejection after another, they chose to keep trying—and failing—rather than seek help, as asking for support triggered memories of those painful school experiences.

Social settings can magnify the challenges of dyslexia, leaving children feeling isolated, misunderstood, and burdened by a quiet fear of being labelled "different." This quiet burden often follows them, shaping their choices and hesitations well into adulthood.

## *The Social and Emotional Aspects of Dyslexia*

The effects of dyslexia go beyond academic difficulties. Research shows children with dyslexia frequently face challenges in their social and emotional development (O'Brien

& Yeatman, 2020). They may develop a negative self-image, feel inadequate compared to their classmates, and fear judgment from their peers, all of which negatively influence their self-esteem. Children who believe they cannot perform as well as others may withdraw from social interactions or feel anxious in new situations. Parents, teachers, and friends can help create supportive environments by understanding these emotional hurdles.

Social and emotional health are often in limbo for children with dyslexia as they experience the constant push and pull of forward progress and stagnating regression. Self-image—a person's perception of themselves—can significantly impact how they view their abilities and inherent value. If a child consistently faces challenges with reading and writing, they may start to see themself as less capable or less intelligent than their peers. This damaging self-perception can result in low self-esteem and a limited mind, which, if not treated, can affect their career, relationships with others, and most importantly, their relationship with themself. They may also avoid participating in group activities or hesitate to make new friends out of fear of rejection or failure.

Focusing on building resilience and self-esteem is essential in countering these negative feelings. Resilience is the ability to bounce back from difficulties, while self-esteem is about feeling good about yourself. Developing these traits can empower children to tackle obstacles head-on and establish a firm belief in their own capabilities. Children who believe in themselves are more likely to try new things, make friends, and enjoy social interactions.

# A Tool Kit for Building Resilience and Self-Esteem in Dyslexic Learners

What steps can we take to build resilience and self-esteem in children with dyslexia? I must reiterate that it's important to celebrate small victories. These children run up against the same struggles day in and day out. Those letters and numbers on the page seem to dance, shift, and wiggle, and no matter how hard the child tries—how closely they pay attention, how much effort they put into doing things "right"—it feels like a losing battle. Even when they finish one reading assignment, the sense of accomplishment fades, overshadowed by the exhaustion from countless moments of struggle throughout the day. Parents and teachers must acknowledge even the smallest achievements, whether reading a single sentence without hesitation or participating in a group discussion. This recognition helps children feel valued. It shows them that they did have successful moments during the day, encouraging them to keep trying.

It's also important to teach children to understand and articulate their dyslexia. Children can better advocate for themselves when they know about their learning differences. Reddit user WeCanAllWin says their parents never talked to them about their dyslexia, dyscalculia, or ADD because they didn't want to hurt their child's feelings (2019). However, this further aggravated WeCanAllWin's frustration growing up. If they had been taught to explain to their friends why they needed extra time on a reading assignment, the transparency could have fostered understanding among their peers and helped them feel empowered instead of humiliated and embarrassed.

Encouraging a growth mindset is also vital. This means teaching children that effort and persistence are crucial for growth. Instead of saying, "I'm not good at this," instruct them to say, "I will keep trying until I improve."

This doesn't mean they should continue using methods that have consistently failed dyslexic learners; instead, they will keep pushing forward, building on their MORE strengths, and aiming to improve daily.

Speech therapist and dyslexia advocate Jeannette Washington suggests the following strategies to help your child become a resilient adult (2023):

- **Identify your child's struggles and seek early intervention:** Identifying dyslexia early can help your child understand how they learn and build foundational reading and writing skills before it becomes an overwhelming problem.

- **View their disabilities as their strengths:** Trust your child's instincts and let them navigate challenges their own way. Skip the "this is how it's done" talk; there's more than one path to growth, and theirs is worth exploring. Celebrate all the ways they are MORE.

- **Build self-esteem:** Praise their achievements and provide positive reinforcement to help them feel proud of themselves and encourage them to persevere through difficulties.

- **Encourage a growth mindset:** Help them see challenges as opportunities for growth rather than mountains whose peaks surpass the clouds.

- **Teach them how to advocate for themself:** Help them understand how they learn. Teach them that it's okay to ask for and receive help, and encourage them to communicate their needs.

- **Partner with academic personnel for a supportive educational environment:** When parents, teachers, and peers understand dyslexia, they provide a safe space for children to thrive and feel valued and accepted. Always offer emotional support, keep lines of communication open, and advocate for your child's needs in their school system.

- **Suggest role models or mentors:** Encourage them to learn about and gain inspiration from successful adults who have overcome dyslexic challenges.

- **Utilize assistive technology:** Text-to-speech software and the reverse, speech-to-text tools, audiobooks, apps, and other technological resources can help level the academic playing field.

- **Participate in resilience-building activities:** Sports, youth theatre, art classes, and extracurricular clubs can help children with dyslexia develop teamwork, self-discipline, and perseverance.

- **Continue to provide guidance during their transition to adulthood:** This stage of life can be daunting for anyone. Please don't leave your child to navigate independent living, post-secondary education, or career choices on their own. Continue to help guide them as they develop self-advocacy skills and confidence in themself.

## Success Stories of Resilience and Support

During my studies, I met **Sam**, an 11-year-old boy who struggled with reading. His parents shared that he'd become withdrawn, shying away from friends. We worked collaboratively with his teacher, Ms. Jones, who introduced Sam to a reading program catered to his dyslexia. Gradually, his reading skills improved, and his newfound confidence spilled over, boosting his reading and helping him step out socially, connect with friends, and share his love for sports.

While volunteering at a school in Toronto, I met **Mia**, a 12-year-old girl who had struggled with dyslexia from an early age. She often felt embarrassed in class, as she lagged behind her peers and needed extra help to keep up with reading and writing. Her parents and I worked together, teaching her how to educate her classmates about dyslexia and how it affected her learning. Feeling empowered, she started a drama club and directed a play that shared her story. Her message reached beyond the classroom, raising awareness and inspiring others to advocate for themselves and their school needs.

Sam and Mia's stories remind us that empowering children with dyslexia isn't about "fixing" them; it's about giving them the skills to face challenges head-on, both in the classroom and beyond.

When we shift our perspective from correcting to equipping, we open the door for them to grow in confidence and self-advocacy.

## Summary

In this chapter, we explored the essential role of parental support in creating a safe and nurturing environment for children with dyslexia at home. We discussed the importance of advocating for their needs in school settings, fostering a dyslexia-friendly atmosphere, and building social and emotional skills. By recognizing their achievements and promoting a growth mindset, you're guiding them to embrace who they are and what they're capable of.

As we move into the final chapter, we'll consider a future of endless possibilities for children with dyslexia, examining how their MORE strengths contribute to shaping a world that thrives on diversity and fresh ideas.

## Chapter 8

# A Future of Endless Possibilities

*For the student, knowing he is dyslexic is empowering ... [It provides him] with self-understanding and self-awareness of what he has and needs to succeed.*
—Sally Shaywitz

If you recall from Chapter 2, the current average lifespan is 76 years for women and 71 for men (*Life Expectancy*, n.d.). This means your child is only under your wing for a small fraction of their life. You have the most influence now, and you must utilize this stage of life to help your child set the foundation for their future.

In recent years, the workplace has changed dramatically. New technologies, remote work, and shifting expectations have reshaped how we approach our jobs. Many companies seek employees who can think creatively and adapt quickly to new challenges. This changing environment has led to a greater recognition of the diverse talents individuals with dyslexia can bring.

Kate Griggs, founder of Made by Dyslexia, and Richard Addison of Ernst & Young Global Limited (EY) understand the value of these minds and the immense innovations they bring to the business world. In their publication, *The Value of Dyslexia*, they state (2018):

The changing world of work requires a transformational approach to how skills and abilities are recognized. A significant change in demand for a balance of skills and abilities means those who work collaboratively and across disciplines will be required in the future... Dyslexic strengths can help meet this business requirement and provide a significant opportunity to harness a different and widely untapped talent pool.

Addison further acknowledges what he calls "huge benefits" by maximizing strengths and "proactively educating, recruiting, developing and retaining those with dyslexia" (Griggs & Addison, 2018). In other words, the evolving job market needs a fresh view on recognizing skills. With a growing demand for collaborative, versatile workers, dyslexic strengths are a valuable and underused asset that could fulfill these needs.

Many businesses have traditionally focused on standardized testing and conventional skills assessment. However, these often emphasize rote memorization and linear problem-solving, which can disadvantage individuals with dyslexia. This focus can overlook creative perspectives, innovative thinking, and problem-solving skills, leaving their talents un-dervalued.

To truly benefit from their skills, we need to change how we view abilities in the workplace.

In this final chapter, we'll discuss the evolving landscape of the modern workplace and what individuals with dyslexia bring to it. We hope to inspire parents, teachers, employers, and kids to recognize and cultivate their abilities so they can excel in the world of work. We'll also examine several careers that would be a good fit for these ingenious, out-of-the-box thinkers who excel at reasoning and expression.

## Jobs Dyslexic Minds Were Built For

Let's look at some job categories that are well-suited for these individuals.

### *Creativity and Design*

Creativity and design careers include graphic, interior, and product design. These jobs allow individuals to express themselves through visual media. Typically, these roles re-quire a strong sense of aesthetics and an aptitude for fresh perspectives. Responsibilities may include creating artwork, developing layouts, and working with clients to bring ideas to life.

These careers are perfect for people with dyslexia because they often rely on visual thinking rather than text-based processing. These individuals may excel in this area because they can see patterns and imagine possibilities. Their unique perspectives and creative approaches could lead to them becoming celebrated designers in their community.

## Healthcare

Healthcare careers, including nursing, physical therapy, and occupational therapy, offer rewarding opportunities for individuals to help others. These roles often require strong interpersonal skills and a solid understanding of human anatomy. Responsibilities may include patient care, treatment planning, and communication with families.

Individuals with dyslexia can thrive in healthcare because they often have strong emotional intelligence and empathy. They may excel at connecting with patients, which is crucial for adequate care.

## Performing and Visual Arts

Careers in performing and visual arts include actors, musicians, and painters. These job roles allow for personal expression and creativity. Typically, these careers require practice, dedication, and performance skills. Responsibilities may include rehearsing for shows, creating art, and engaging with audiences.

Performance-driven careers can be ideal for individuals with dyslexia due to their strong creative abilities and hands-on skills. Through their art, they may find their strength in storytelling and creating emotional connections.

Reflect on young John Lennon, a musician with dyslexia who crafted songs that touched listeners profoundly and continue to shape lives over 40 years after his untimely passing.

Also, remember Jay Leno, an actor and comedian with dyslexia who reigned over late-night television for years. His talent for storytelling and engaging audiences helped him connect with fans and receive critical acclaim.

## Hospitality

The hospitality industry includes jobs such as hotel management, event planning, and restaurant services. These roles require excellent customer service skills and managing various tasks. Employees often work in dynamic environments, dealing with customer needs and ensuring satisfaction.

Individuals with dyslexia often thrive in hospitality due to their strong interpersonal skills and ability to think on their feet. They can also usually remember faces and details, which is beneficial in customer-oriented roles.

## Fashion and Styling

Fashion and styling careers include fashion designer, stylist, and merchandiser roles. These jobs often require a keen eye for trends and an understanding of aesthetics. Responsibilities may include designing clothing, advising customers on styles, and managing retail displays.

Individuals with dyslexia may find this field appealing due to their adventurous thinking and creativity. They often have a unique style perspective that can set trends. A stylist with dyslexia who has a knack for mixing and matching styles in ways that surprise and delight clients may find themself featured in prominent fashion shows.

## Sports

Careers in sports encompass roles like coaching, sports management, and athletics. These positions require teamwork, physical fitness, and strategic thinking. Responsibilities may include training athletes, organizing events, and promoting teams.

Individuals with dyslexia often excel in sports due to their ability to think strategically and read body language. They may find physical expression and teamwork more natural than written communication.

Joe Whitt Jr., the defensive coordinator for the Washington Commanders NFL football team, has dyslexia and is a coach with a remarkable ability to inspire and motivate athletes. He has served in various professional coaching positions with his alma mater, Auburn University, and several NFL teams, including the Green Bay Packers and Dallas Cowboys. His skills in understanding player dynamics and fostering a positive team environment contribute to his continued success.

## Social Work

Social work careers involve advocating for individuals and communities. Social workers often help people navigate challenges in their lives. Requirements in this field include strong communication skills and connecting with diverse populations.

Social work can be fulfilling for individuals with dyslexia as it caters to their empathetic nature and problem-solving skills. Their ability to see the bigger picture and understand emotional needs can make them effective in this field.

## *Sales and Marketing*

Sales and marketing roles involve promoting products and services. These careers require persuasive communication skills and an understanding of consumer behaviour. Responsibilities can include conducting market research, developing campaigns, and interacting with clients.

Individuals with dyslexia often excel at reading social cues and understanding what drives people, which can be a significant advantage in sales and marketing. This intuitive sense of what resonates with others allows them to connect more profoundly with clients, fostering trust and building lasting customer relationships.

## *Construction*

Careers in construction include roles like contractor, architect, and site manager. These positions often require physical skills, planning, project management, and special awareness. Responsibilities include coordinating tasks, managing budgets, and ensuring safety standards.

Individuals with dyslexia may thrive in construction due to their strong spatial awareness and hands-on skills. They often excel at visualizing projects and understanding how things fit together.

## Landscaping and Gardening

Landscaping and gardening careers involve creating and maintaining outdoor spaces. Roles can include landscape designer, gardener, or horticulturist. These jobs often require creativity, knowledge of plants, and physical work. Responsibilities include designing gardens, planting, and caring for plants.

Landscaping is a natural fit for individuals with dyslexia. It combines hands-on creativity with real-world problem-solving. Their knack for working with their hands and seeing natural patterns creates stunning designs that speak for themselves.

## Entrepreneurship

Entrepreneurship involves starting and managing a business. Entrepreneurs often take risks to bring their ideas to life. Responsibilities can include managing finances, marketing products, and networking.

Many individuals with dyslexia excel in entrepreneurship thanks to their creative problem-solving and risk-taking abilities. Their fresh perspectives often lead to unconventional business ideas that stand out in the market.

Richard Branson has succeeded tremendously in multiple business endeavours, from recording studios to space travel! His creative solutions and determination have helped him overcome obstacles and achieve much more than many people dream of doing.

These careers are just a glimpse of what's possible—your child can excel in many other fields, too. Allowing them to explore their career interests can make all the difference. When parents impose their own ambitions, children can feel boxed in, potentially damaging their self-worth and eroding trust in their relationship with you. Instead, encourage them to follow what excites them—it helps them develop a strong sense of identity and builds a lasting, open bond with you.

## Preparing Dyslexic Minds to Excel in Society

Here are some areas that individuals with dyslexia may navigate differently as they prepare to enter the workforce:

- **Verbal communication:** Those with dyslexia might struggle to express themselves verbally when presenting ideas or participating in discussions. They may need help communicating their ideas or speaking fluently under pressure.

- **Written communication:** Some might find it overwhelming to write emails or reports. They could have trouble with spelling, grammar, or organizing their thoughts on paper, leading to frustration and anxiety, especially when conveying important information.

- **Following instructions:** If a task involves multiple steps, they may find it challenging to remember each part. They might forget key components or mix them up, compromising the quality of their work.

- **Organization:** Many find it hard to keep their workspace orderly, leading to confusion and increased stress. Energy and engagement levels can also fluctuate. Some may feel exhausted by the effort required to keep up with their peers.

- **Information overload:** In environments filled with data and constant communication, information overload can be overstimulating, making it hard to focus on and process relevant information. Long and overly complicated meetings can add to this frustration, as it can be arduous to maintain attention for extended periods.

## How Parents and Teachers Can Help Develop Workplace Readiness

Parents and teachers are the launchpad that propels a child with dyslexia toward future success. Imagine a rocket preparing for takeoff: without a solid base and suitable support systems, it can't lift off. But with every bit of encouragement and belief in their abilities, that rocket gains the fuel it needs to soar. The steady, intentional support from home and school ignites a child's confidence, preparing them to break barriers and reach new heights in the workforce.

Parents help build that launchpad not by shielding children from every obstacle but by equipping them with the skills to overcome them independently. Encouraging small habits that imply healthy risk-taking, self-advocacy, and goal-setting tasks strengthens this foundation, fueling confidence and self-reliance. When the rocket finally takes off, it does so with the power to navigate challenges and reach new heights.

Teachers build on this foundation set by parents by fostering exploration and discovery in the classroom. With hands-on activities and collaborative projects, they encourage students to try different approaches, helping them understand how they learn best. This process supports academic growth and equips students with essential skills they'll carry into the workplace.

## *How Employers Can Ready the Workplace*

Employers should consider implementing alternative assessment methods that highlight creativity and collaboration. This could involve practical tasks that allow individuals to showcase their strengths in real-world scenarios rather than relying solely on written tests. By doing so, companies can create an inclusive environment that values diverse ways of thinking.

Inclusive hiring practices don't just look good on paper—they bring in untapped talent. By partnering with educational institutions and dyslexia advocacy groups, companies can reach candidates who see things differently. And trust me, those fresh perspectives? They might be the next big thing.

Creating a supportive environment enhances the overall workplace culture. Employers should create spaces where employees feel comfortable sharing their ups and downs without getting ridiculed. For example, regular feedback sessions and open communication can encourage employees to voice their needs.

Workshops that emphasize team-building and diverse work styles offer employers real advantages. By fostering team bonding, companies can leverage the unique strengths of all employees, including those with dyslexia.

## *Work Smarter, Not Harder*

Using the following strategies can help navigate the workplace more effectively:

- **Assistive technology:** Speech-to-text software ensures individuals with dyslexia focus on their ideas and contributions without getting caught up in the technicalities of written expression. Allowing them to dictate their thoughts instead of typing relieves the stress of spelling and grammar, making it faster and more comfortable to organize ideas, respond to emails, and prepare reports.

- **Visual organization tools:** Tools like colour-coded charts—such as project timelines with colour distinctions for priority levels—and digital planners, like apps that set reminders for deadlines or recurring tasks, can simplify complex workflows by breaking them into manageable steps. These visual aids help track progress, making it easier to stay focused and organized.

- **Workplace accommodations and modifications:** Discuss workspace adjustments or task modifications with your employers, such as flexible deadlines or more structured instructions. Employers must see these accommodations not as perks but as essential tools that empower individuals with dyslexia to perform at their full potential.

- **Proficiency in common office software:** Knowledge of digital platforms such as Microsoft Office or Google Workplace is a requirement of many jobs. Effective communication and teamwork training sessions can offer valuable experience in a supportive setting.

- **Role-playing scenarios:** Engaging in mock interviews or presentations can prepare for real-life experiences. Getting comfortable with everyday workplace situations can ease anxiety and bolster confidence.

- **Networking:** Connecting with mentors or peers who understand these experiences can provide support and guidance during the job search process. Many organizations focus on helping individuals with dyslexia find employment opportunities by providing resources and connections to navigate the job market effectively.

- **Asking for help when needed:** As previously noted, advocating for and articulating specific workplace needs is essential, enabling employers to make the necessary adjustments for optimal performance.

As your child matures, introduce them to tools and strategies that build on their MORE strengths, empowering them to work smarter and inspiring them to reach new heights.

## Summary

Parents have a brief, powerful window to help shape their children's future. This time can lay the groundwork for endless possibilities—or close doors. It all hinges on how you love, guide, and support them now. This foundation becomes even more essential as today's workplace evolves, increasingly valuing creative and adaptable thinkers.

In this chapter, we addressed the modern workplace and the qualities individuals with dyslexia can offer. We explored various job categories, looked at how parents, teachers, and children can prepare for future workplace readiness, and examined how employers can embrace workers with diverse thinking, learning, and processing skills. Children with dyslexia don't need to "overcome" their differences—they need a world that values them. As more companies recognize the power of diverse thinking, the future workforce is shifting. What's being built today is a foundation for a workplace that doesn't just accommodate differences but thrives on them.

# Spill the (Alphabet) Soup

## – Leave a Review!

Well, look at that—you've almost reached the finish line! Whether you powered through or savored every page, your journey here matters.

If this book sparked a new understanding, gave you a "light-bulb moment," or simply helped you feel seen, sharing a review would mean the world. Your words can encourage other parents, teachers, and advocates to pick this up and start making a difference in the lives of children with dyslexia.

Ready to be someone's hidden hero? Just scan the QR code below. It will only take a minute or two!

 Note: If the QR code doesn't work, please visit the Amazon marketplace where you purchased the book. Scroll to the bottom of the book's product page and click on **'Write a customer review'** to leave your feedback manually. Thank you for your support! Grateful for you... even if we spell it **"graetful"** sometimes!

# Conclusion

As we journeyed through the stories of Clayton, Christian, and many others who navigate the world with dyslexia each day, we peeled back the layers of this often misunderstood condition. Through their eyes, we discovered not a disability but a powerful, unique way of thinking—a "superability" that defies convention. With each story, the hope has been to broaden the world's perspective, inviting a deeper, more compassionate understanding of what it truly means to live—and thrive—with dyslexia.

In EMPOWERING DYSLEXIA: PROVEN TOOLS & STRATEGIES FOR PARENTS & TEACHERS TO FOSTER READING & INSPIRE DYSLEXIC BRILLIANCE IN CHILDREN, we introduced the MORE framework—a transformative shift in perspective that allows us to see dyslexia through a new lens. This framework gives children the tools to thrive in a world that has long labelled them "different." By reframing their narrative, we hand them the keys to unlock doors that were once closed, empowering them to navigate challenges with resilience, confidence, and the unique brilliance they bring.

With creative ingenuity, out-of-the-box thinking, distinctive reasoning, and expressive brilliance, these individuals transform challenges into stepping stones. Their strengths don't just help them navigate the obstacles dyslexia presents; they fuel their journey toward academic achievement, personal growth, and a life of limitless potential.

In these pages, we discussed the pivotal role of parental support in nurturing a safe and encouraging atmosphere for children within the family. This book also emphasized the importance of advocating for a child's educational needs, creating a dyslexia-supportive school environment, nurturing social and emotional skills, celebrating achievements, and fostering a growth mindset. It highlighted that with the right interventions and encouragement, dyslexic learners can flourish and emerge as resilient individuals.

We also highlighted the importance of building a solid foundation for your child's future—a future where they can thrive in a rapidly evolving workplace. With technological advancements and the rise of remote work, today's job market values creativity and adaptable talent. Throughout this journey, we delved into the modern job landscape and the valuable contributions those with dyslexia bring to it. We explored career paths that align with their strengths and identified practical strategies that parents, educators, and children can use to boost readiness for the workplace.

As awareness of dyslexia expands, workplaces are increasingly adapting to embrace diverse learning and working styles. Each step today lays the groundwork for a future workforce that values diversity and harnesses it to fuel innovation.

We hope this journey has given you valuable insight into the unique workings of your child's dyslexic mind. With this new understanding, may you feel ready to support them as they step into their future—prepared, encouraged, and empowered by their MORE abilities. Together, let's nurture their determination, resilience, and boundless potential for greatness.

As we conclude this book, let's look at where Clayton's path has led him. From a young boy who struggled to keep up in class, he's now a college graduate with a degree from Texas Tech, leading business teams and excelling in his career. Recently, he stepped into a higher role with more pay, influence, and responsibility—a testament to his resilience. But Clayton's dreams don't stop there. He hopes to purchase property one day and develop an institution that embraces and empowers young minds who learn differently. He imagines a school where children can freely explore how they think and learn, discovering their brilliance without the weight of judgment, ridicule, or special treatment. His dream is a world where learning and thinking differently isn't just welcomed—it's the standard.

Though I'm no longer in contact with Christian, the work I established with his school administration and the counsellors who remained in Venezuela made a difference. It opened the door to a new understanding of a learning difference they had not encountered before. I'm hopeful the tools and resources we introduced for Christian didn't just boost his learning and self-esteem—they rekindled his love for school. Now, I picture him walking through those classroom doors with a spark of excitement, eager to embrace the journey he once dreaded.

Christian taught me more than I could have ever teach him. He showed me resilience, how to find light even when things feel heavy, and the quiet power of believing in yourself when the world doesn't always see you. His journey reminded me that every child, especially those with dyslexia, has lessons of their own to share with us—lessons of courage, patience, and self-acceptance. I hope these pages have kindled in you that same determination to walk beside your child with love, confidence, and an open heart, embracing the beauty in every challenge.

# About The Author

A. Marie doesn't have dyslexia, but growing up with ADHD taught her early on what it feels like to navigate a world that doesn't quite fit. For her, the classroom was often a place of frustration rather than discovery, where being "different" felt more like a burden than a gift. These early challenges sparked a lifelong passion for understanding how unique minds work—and how they can thrive when given the right support.

Over the years, she has had the privilege of working with children who remind her so much of her younger self. Children like Christian, who rediscovered his confidence after learning strategies tailored to his dyslexia, and Mia, who turned her struggles into strengths by educating her peers about learning differences. Their journeys—marked by resilience, brilliance, and the determination to be understood—continue to inspire her every day.

With a degree in Psychology and extensive experience working closely with children, A. Marie's journey has been guided by a simple belief: every child deserves to be celebrated for their strengths, not limited by their struggles. She has devoted her efforts to helping families, educators, and kids transform challenges into opportunities for growth. Drawing from her own experiences and the invaluable lessons learned from working with remarkable young minds, she aims to equip parents and teachers with practical tools and strategies to help every child thrive.

This book is a heartfelt offering to those parents staring at a blank page, wondering how to help the world see their child as they do: full of possibility, promise, and brilliance. Through her work, she invites readers to join her in celebrating the power of being different.

# References

Adrija. (2021, June 1). Which diamond cut has the most facets? *Miorola Jewellery*. https://miorola.com/blog/which-diamond-cut-has-the-most-facets

Arthur, A. (2022, June 24). Dyslexia isn't a disorder, it's essential to how our species adapt, say researchers. *BBC Science Focus Magazine*. https://www.sciencefocus.com/news/dyslexia-isnt-a-disorder-its-part-of-our-species-cultural-evolution-say-researchers

Beamish, B. (2023, September 20). *These are the best jobs for a dyslexic*. Dyslexia Octopus. https://dyslexiaoctopus.com/best-jobs-for-a-dyslexic/

*Best jobs for dyslexics (adults) - top 10 in 2024*. (n.d.). My Disability Jobs. https://mydisabilityjobs.com/jobs-for-dyslexics/

*Boost your brain with DYNSEO*. (n.d.). DYNSEO. https://www.dynseo.com/en/

Borleffs, E., Maassen, B. A. M., Lyytinen, H., & Zwarts, F. (2019). Cracking the code: The impact of orthographic transparency and morphological-syllabic complexity on reading and developmental dyslexia. *Frontiers in Psychology*, *9*. https://doi.org/10.3389/fpsyg.2018.02534

Brooks, R., & Archey, X. (2022). Building resilience and self-esteem for students with and without disabilities: A reference trifold for K-12 educators. In *California*

*State University San Marcos*. https://scholarworks.calstate.edu/downloads/q524 jw11g

Butcher, H. (2021, February 12). Dyslexia and emotional intelligence. *Dyslexia the Gift Blog*. https://blog.dyslexia.com/dyslexia-and-emotional-intelligence/

Cambridge Dictionary. (n.d.-a). Ingenuity. In *CambridgeDictionary.org dictionary*. Retrieved July 22, 2024, from https://dictionary.cambridge.org/us/dictionary/e nglish/ingenuity

Cambridge Dictionary. (n.d.-b). Multifaceted. In *CambridgeDictionary.org dictio‐ nary*. Retrieved July 22, 2024, from https://dictionary.cambridge.org/us/diction ary/english/multifaceted

Cancer, A., Manzoli, S., & Antonietti, A. (2016). The alleged link between creativity and dyslexia: Identifying the specific process in which dyslexic students excel. *Cogent Psychology*, *3*(1). https://doi.org/10.1080/23311908.2016.1190309

Cardine, T. (2023a). *Master secure attachment: The key to raising happy, well adjust‐ ed, and thriving children*. Independently published. https://a.co/d/3Pb6aow

Cardine, T. (2023b). *Solutions to common parenting dilemmas: Answers to issues that drive moms and dads crazy*. Independently published. https://a.co/d/0CT5oh8

Carioti, D., Masia, M. F., Travellini, S., & Berlingeri, M. (2021). Orthographic depth and developmental dyslexia: a meta-analytic study. *Annals of Dyslexia*, *71*, 399–428. https://doi.org/10.1007/s11881-021-00226-0

Carson, J. (2020). *Why is creativity important and what does it contribute?* National Youth Council of Ireland. https://www.youth.ie/articles/why-is-creativity-import ant-and-what-does-it-contribute/

Cherry, K. (2023, February 28). *Overview of VARK learning styles*. Verywell Mind. https://www.verywellmind.com/vark-learning-styles-2795156

Cleveland Clinic. (n.d.-a). *Dyscalculia*. https://my.clevelandclinic.org/health/dise ases/23949-dyscalculia

Cleveland Clinic. (n.d.-b). *Dysgraphia*. https://my.clevelandclinic.org/health/dise ases/23294-dysgraphia

Cleveland Clinic. (n.d.-c). *Dyslexia*. https://my.clevelandclinic.org/health/disease s/6005-dyslexia

Cole, C. (2019, November). *Strengths of dyslexia*. Dyslexia Support South. https://www.dyslexiasupportsouth.org.nz/parent-toolkit/emotional-imp act/strengths-of-dyslexia/

Cole, C. (2020, January 28). *Five stages of dyslexia self-acceptance*. Learning Differ‐ ences Aotearoa Trust. https://www.learningdifferences.org.nz/presenter-notes /five-stages-of-dyslexia-self-acceptance

Crockett, K. (n.d.). *Jay Leno, comedian & television personality*. The Yale Center for Dyslexia & Creativity. https://dyslexia.yale.edu/story/jay-leno/

The Cross-Eyed Pianist. (2018, November 4). *My child & dyslexia: A parent's per‐ spective*. The Cross-Eyed Pianist. https://crosseyedpianist.com/2018/11/04/my -child-dyslexia-a-parents-perspective/

Cullins, A. (2022, October 22). Key strategies to teach children empathy (sorted by age). *Big Life Journal*. https://biglifejournal.com/blogs/blog/key-strategies-tea ch-children-empathy

Davis, R. D. (2010). *The gift of dyslexia: Why some of the smartest people can't read...and how they can learn*. Perigree Books. https://www.dyslexia.com/book /the-gift-of-dyslexia/

Denton, C. A., Montroy, J. J., Zucker, T. A., & Cannon, G. (2020). Designing an inter‐ vention in reading and self-regulation for students with significant reading difficulties, including dyslexia. *Learning Disability Quarterly*, *44*(3), 073194871989947. https://doi.org/10.1177/0731948719899479

*Diagnosis - Dyslexia*. (2023, July 12). National Health Services UK. https://www.nhs.uk/conditions/dyslexia/diagnosis/

Dollosa, S. (2021, September 13). 41 dyslexia quotes to inspire you. *Bookbot*. https://www.bookbotkids.com/blog/dyslexia-quotes

Douce, D. (2022, August 16). *Advocating for students with dyslexia in public schools*. International Dyslexia Association. https://dyslexiaida.org/advocating-for-a-child-with-dyslexia-within-the-public-education-system/

Douce, D. (2023, March 11). *Social and emotional problems related to dyslexia*. International Dyslexia Association. https://dyslexiaida.org/social-emotional/

Duboc, V., Dufourcq, P., Blader, P., & Roussigné, M. (2015). Asymmetry of the brain: Development and implications. *Annual Review of Genetics*, *49*(1), 647–672. https://doi.org/10.1146/annurev-genet-112414-055322

*Dyslexia*. (n.d.-a). National Health Services UK. https://www.nhs.uk/conditions/Dyslexia

Dyslexia. (n.d.-b). *Psychology Today*. https://www.psychologytoday.com/us/conditions/dyslexia

*Dyslexia and the brain*. (n.d.). International Dyslexia Association. https://dyslexiaida.org/dyslexia-and-the-brain-fact-sheet/

*Dyslexia FAQ*. (n.d.). The Yale Center for Dyslexia & Creativity. https://www.dyslexia.yale.edu/dyslexia/dyslexia-faq/

*Dyslexia-friendly environment*. (n.d.). The Yale Center for Dyslexia & Creativity. https://dyslexia.yale.edu/dyslexia/dyslexia-friendly-environment/

*Dyslexia in the workplace.* (n.d.). Cognassist. https://cognassist.com/insights/dyslexia-in-the-workplace/

*Dyslexia myths and facts.* (n.d.). University of Michigan. https://dyslexiahelp.umich.edu/dyslexics/learn-about-dyslexia/what-is-dyslexia/dyslexia-myths-and-facts

The Edublox Team. (2023, June 30). *11 dyslexia success stories of children and students.* Edublox Online Tutor. https://www.edubloxtutor.com/dyslexia-success-stories/

Eide, B. L., & Eide, F. F. (2011). *The dyslexic advantage.* Penguin.

Embracing my dyslexia: A journey of acceptance. (n.d.). *Blogs.Lboro.* https://blog.lboro.ac.uk/edi/2021/10/07/embracing-my-dyslexia-a-journey-of-acceptance/

Enable children to reason logically and critically. (n.d.). *98th Percentile.* https://www.98thpercentile.com/blog/importance-of-logical-reasoning-cognitive-ability-critical-thinking/

Fink, R. (n.d.). *Successful careers: The secrets of adults with dyslexia.* Career Planning and Adult Development Network. https://dyslexiahelp.umich.edu/sites/default/files/SuccessfulCareersDyslexiaFink_1.pdf

5 ways to encourage creativity in kids with dyslexia. (n.d.). *Brain Balance.* https://www.brainbalancecenters.com/blog/ways-encourage-creativity-kids-dyslexia

*A 504 plan for those with dyslexia.* (2019, January 15). Orton Gillingham Online Academy. https://ortongillinghamonlinetutor.com/504-plan-dyslexia/

FOKP. (2021, February 22). *How to develop logic and reasoning skills in kids.* Focus on Kids Pediatrics. https://www.focusonkidspeds.com/info-articles/how-to-develop-logic-and-reasoning-skills-in-kids/

Gamma, E. (2023, October 20). *Left brain vs. right brain: Hemisphere function*. Simply Psychology. https://www.simplypsychology.org/left-brain-vs-right-brain.html

Ghosh, D. (2021, December 30). Exercises to help your child develop reasoning skills. *Hindustan Times School*. https://htschool.hindustantimes.com/editorsdesk/lifeskills/5-exercises-to-build-reasoning-skills-for-kids

Gibbons, R. (n.d.). *From dyslexia to dreams - A parent's story*. LD Online. https://www.ldonline.org/your-stories/personal-stories/dyslexia-dreams-parents-story

Gilbert, N. (2017, March 10). *Supporting students with dyslexia in the home environment*. International School Parent. https://www.internationalschoolparent.com/articles/supporting-students-dyslexia-home-environment/

Giovagnoli, G., Vicari, S., Tomassetti, S., & Menghini, D. (2016). The role of visual-spatial abilities in dyslexia: Age differences in children's reading? *Frontiers in Psychology*, 7. https://doi.org/10.3389/fpsyg.2016.01997

Gobbo, K. (2020). *Dyslexia and creativity*. Cambridge Scholars Publishing. https://www.cambridgescholars.com/resources/pdfs/978-1-5275-4216-7-sample.pdf

Griggs, K. (2022a, September 23). *5 reasons dyslexics make skilled communicators*. LinkedIn. https://www.linkedin.com/pulse/5-reasons-dyslexics-make-skilled-communicators-kate-griggs/

Griggs, K. (2022b, November 25). Tips and strategies for working with dyslexia. *Harvard Business Review*. https://hbr.org/2022/11/tips-and-strategies-for-working-with-dyslexia

Griggs, K., & Addison, R. (2018). *The value of dyslexia: Dyslexic strengths and the changing world of work*. Ernst & Young. https://assets.ey.com/content/dam/ey-sites/ey-com/en_uk/topics/diversity/ey-the-value-of-dyslexia-dyslexic-strengths-and-the-changing-world-of-work.pdf

Gutiérrez-Ortega, M., Torres-Quesada, M., Crespo, P., López-Fernández, V., Far-iña, N., & Barbón, A. (2023). Are dyslexic people more creative? Myth or reality: A meta-analysis. *Psicología Educativa, 29*(1), 55–64. https://www.redalyc.org/journal/6137/613775169006/html/

Guy-Evans, O. (2021, May 18). *Lateralization of brain function.* Simply Psychology. https://www.simplypsychology.org/brain-lateralization.html

Haft, S., & Hoeft, F. (2019, December). *What protective factors lead to resilience in students with dyslexia?* International Dyslexia Association. https://dyslexiaida.org/what-protective-factors-lead-to-resilience-in-students-with-dyslexia/

*History of Davis methods.* (2023, September 28). Davis Dyslexia Association International. https://www.dyslexia.com/davis-difference/about-davis/davis-program-history/history-of-davis-programs/

Homer-Dixon, T. F. (2002). *The ingenuity gap: facing the economic, environmental, and other challenges of an increasingly complex and unpredictable world.* Vintage Books. https://a.co/d/76C3WZ5.

How, L. (2022, May 10). *10 tips for dyslexic friendly classrooms.* TeacherToolkit. https://www.teachertoolkit.co.uk/2022/05/05/dyslexic-friendly-classrooms/

Howley-Rouse, A. (2020, October 19). *A strengths-based approach to teaching neurodiverse learners.* The Education Hub. https://theeducationhub.org.nz/a-strengths-based-approach-to-teaching-diverse-learners/

Hudson, R. F., High, L., & Al Otaiba, S. (n.d.). *Dyslexia and the brain: What does current research tell us?* Reading Rockets. https://www.readingrockets.org/topics/dyslexia/articles/dyslexia-and-brain-what-does-current-research-tell-us

Human ingenuity is your most strategic asset. (2017, October 17). *IE University Lifelong Learning.* https://www.ie.edu/lifelong-learning/blog/innovation/human-ingenuity-strategic-asset/

*The IEP process: Everything you need to know.* (n.d.). University of Michigan Dyslexia Help. https://dyslexiahelp.umich.edu/parents/living-with-dyslexia/school/iep-process-everything-you-need-to-know

Ihbour, S., Anarghou, H., Boulhana, A., Najimi, M., & Chigr, F. (2021). Mental health among students with neurodevelopment disorders: case of dyslexic children and adolescents. *Dementia & Neuropsychologia, 15*(4), 533–540. https://doi.org/10.1590/1980-57642021dn15-040014

*Independent teacher training programs accredited by IDA.* (n.d.). International Dyslexia Association. https://dyslexiaida.org/accredited-teaching-training-programs/

*Intervention strategies.* (n.d.). Dyslexia SPELD Foundation. https://dsf.net.au/effective-remediation

Ismail, A. S., & Zulkurnain, N. S. Z. (2019). The role of environment as third teacher towards the development of educational space for dyslexic children. *International Journal of Built Environment and Sustainability, 6*(2), 51–62. https://doi.org/10.11113/ijbes.v6.n2.356

James, C. (2018, September 5). The beauty of being different. *Tiny Buddha.* https://tinybuddha.com/blog/the-beauty-of-being-different/

Karczewski, S. A. (2022, November 16). *7 tips for coping with your child's unexpected diagnosis.* Children's Hospital of California. https://health.choc.org/coping-tips-unexpected-diagnosis/

Kearns, D. M., Hancock, R., Hoeft, F., Pugh, K. R., & Frost, S. J. (2019). The Neurobiology of Dyslexia. *TEACHING Exceptional Children, 51*(3), 175–188. https://doi.org/10.1177/0040059918820051

Kumar, J. (2019, September 3). The famous faces of dyslexia. *Junior Learning USA.* https://juniorlearning.com/blogs/news/the-famous-faces-of-dyslexia

Lachmann, T., & Bergström, K. (2023). Developmental dyslexia and culture: The impact of writing system and orthography. *Journal of Cultural Cognitive Science*, 7(2), 63–69. https://doi.org/10.1007/s41809-023-00129-z

LDAOeng. (2016, January 8). *Success story: Abigail*. Learning Disabilities Association of Ontario. https://www.ldatschool.ca/success-story-abigail-2/

Lennon, J. (n.d.). *John Lennon quotes*. Goodreads. https://www.goodreads.com/quotes/188330-people-like-me-are-aware-of-their-so-called-genius-at

*Life expectancy of the world population*. (n.d.). Worldometer. https://www.worldometers.info/demographics/life-expectancy/

Marianne. (n.d.-a). *How accepting your child's learning differences changes everything*. Homeschooling With Dyslexia. https://homeschoolingwithdyslexia.com/accepting-childs-dyslexia/

Marianne. (n.d.-b). *The strengths of dyslexia*. Homeschooling With Dyslexia. https://homeschoolingwithdyslexia.com/the-strengths-of-dyslexia/

Marshall, A. (2015). *What dyslexics see*. Davis Dyslexia Association International. https://www.dyslexia.com/question/what-dyslexics-see/

Marshall, A. (2019, March 13). Research shows greater improvement from strength-based teaching. *Dyslexia the Gift Blog*. https://blog.dyslexia.com/improvement-strength-based-teaching/

Matta, A. (2019, January 14). *What's it like to live with: A child with dyslexia*. The SWDL. https://www.theswaddle.com/whats-it-like-to-live-with-a-child-with-dyslexia

Mayo Clinic Staff. (2022, August 6). *Dyslexia*. Mayo Clinic. https://www.mayoclinic.org/diseases-conditions/dyslexia/symptoms-causes/syc-20353552

McDonough, M. (2023, December). Dyslexia and the developing brain. *Harvard Medicine Magazine*. https://magazine.hms.harvard.edu/articles/dyslexia-and-developing-brain

Meherally, S. (2022, March 2). What it means to truly "think outside the box." *Harvard Business Review*. https://hbr.org/2022/03/what-it-means-to-truly-think-outside-the-box

Merriam-Webster. (n.d.). Dyslexia. In *Merriam-Webster.com dictionary*. Retrieved July 8, 2024, from https://www.merriam-webster.com/dictionary/dyslexia

Mind Tools Content Team. (n.d.). *VAK learning styles*. Mind Tools. https://www.mindtools.com/ak6cyjn/vak-learning-styles

Morin, A. (n.d.). *11 great quotes about dyslexia*. Understood. https://www.understood.org/en/articles/great-quotes-about-dyslexia

Morin, A. (2024, April 30). *7 common myths about dyslexia*. Understood. https://www.understood.org/en/articles/common-myths-about-dyslexia-reading-issues

MSL Centre Pte Ltd. (2023, February 12). *How to foster a dyslexia friendly environment at home*. LinkedIn. https://www.linkedin.com/pulse/how-foster-dyslexia-friendly-environment-home-msl-centre-pte-ltd/

Mukherjee, R. (2013, March 1). Different is beautiful. *Wisdom Times*. https://www.wisdomtimes.com/blog/different-is-beautiful/

*Multisensory learning*. (n.d.). The Reading Well. https://www.dyslexia-reading-well.com/multisensory-learning.html

Munzer, T., Hussain, K., & Soares, N. (2020). Dyslexia: neurobiology, clinical features, evaluation and management. *Translational Pediatrics*, *9*(S1), S36–S45. https://doi.org/10.21037/tp.2019.09.07

Murrihy, C. (2022, November 7). *How to help your child come to terms with a serious diagnosis.* Irish Society for the Prevention of Cruelty to Children. https://www.is pcc.ie/5-ways-to-help-your-child-come-to-terms-with-a-life-changing-diagnosis/

muskalo. (2024, March 30). *I just want to talk about my experience with dyslexia* [Online forum post]. Reddit. https://www.reddit.com/r/Dyslexia/comments/1br fsoh/i_just_want_to_talk_about_my_experience_with/

*9 quotes about dyslexia.* (n.d.). Touch-Type Read and Spell (TTRS). https://www.r eadandspell.com/us/quotes-about-dyslexia

Nixon, G. (2019, December 3). 8 life hacks for people with dyslexia. *Gemm Learning.* https://www.gemmlearning.com/blog/dyslexia/dyslexia-hacks/

Nunez, K. (2022, July 12). *A guide to helping children with dyslexia outside of school.* Healthline. https://www.healthline.com/health/how-to-help-a-child-with-dyslex ia-at-home

O'Brien, G., & Yeatman, J. D. (2020). Bridging sensory and language theories of dyslexia: Toward a multifactorial model. *Developmental Science, 24*(3). https://d oi.org/10.1111/desc.13039

O'Brien, T. (2020). *Understanding the socio-emotional impact of dyslexia in the inclusive classroom.* IntechOpen. https://www.intechopen.com/chapters/73587

Paphitis, T. (2017, October 4). *Those with dyslexia don't just think outside the box, they build a new one...* LinkedIn. https://www.linkedin.com/pulse/those-dyslexia -dont-just-think-outside-box-build-new-one-paphitis/

Parenting style test. (n.d.). *Psychology Today.* https://www.psychologytoday.com /us/tests/personality/parenting-style-test

Pearce, B. (n.d.). *Confessions of a parent of two dyslexics.* The Yale Center for Dyslexia & Creativity. https://dyslexia.yale.edu/resources/parents/stories-from -parents/confessions-of-a-parent/

Piersol, J. (2024, April 15). Teaching strategies for students with dyslexia. *American University School of Education*. https://soeonline.american.edu/blog/teaching-st rategies-students-with-dyslexia/

plutolympics. (2020, August 21). *Does anyone share my experience of growing up with dyslexia?* [Online forum post]. Reddit. https://www.reddit.com/r/Dyslexia/c omments/ie7lb9/does_anyone_share_my_experience_of_growing_up/

Positive Action Staff. (2022, March 6). How to teach students with dyslexia? 14 evidence-based tips. *Positive Action*. https://www.positiveaction.net/blog/how-t o-teach-students-with-dyslexia

Price, K. M., Wigg, K. G., Misener, V. L., Clarke, A., Yeung, N., Blokland, K., Wilkin⁻ son, M., Kerr, E. N., Guger, S. L., Lovett, M. W., & Barr, C. L. (2021). Language diffi⁻ culties in school-aged children with developmental dyslexia. *Journal of Learning Disabilities*, *55*(3). https://doi.org/10.1177/00222194211006207

*Radiant cut diamond guide*. (2020, July 28). Cape Diamonds. https://www.capedi amonds.co.za/diamond-info/radiant-cut/

Reading comprehension: Why early dyslexia Intervention matters. (2023, August 9). *GoLexic*. https://www.golexic.com/blog/reading-comprehension-and-dyslexi a/

*Reasonable adjustments in the workplace*. (n.d.). British Dyslexia Associa⁻ tion. https://www.bdadyslexia.org.uk/advice/employers/how-can-i-support-my -dyslexic-employees/reasonable-adjustments-in-the-workplace

Reljic, T. (2015, February 2). Dyslexia: Thinking outside the box. *Malta To⁻ day*. https://www.maltatoday.com.mt/lifestyle/health/49663/dyslexia_thinking_ outside_the_box

Resnick, M. (2020, March 31). *10 tips for cultivating creativity in your kids*. Ideas.t ed.com. https://ideas.ted.com/10-tips-for-cultivating-creativity-in-your-kids/

Roell, K. (2019, June 23). *Understanding visual, auditory, and kinesthetic learning styles*. ThoughtCo. https://www.thoughtco.com/three-different-learning-styles-3212040

Roell, K. (2024, August 31). *The kinesthetic learning style: Traits and study strategies*. ThoughtCo. https://www.thoughtco.com/the-kinesthetic-learning-style-3212046

Romero, E. (2024, April 3). *How a student with dyslexia changed my teaching career (and my life)*. Understood. https://www.understood.org/en/articles/how-a-student-with-dyslexia-changed-my-teaching-career-and-my-life

Romero, Y. (2020). Lazy or dyslexic: A multisensory approach to face English language learning difficulties. *English Language Teaching, 13*(5), 34–48. https://eric.ed.gov/?id=EJ1252542

rosie-skies. (2023, November 28). *I'm a reading teacher for middle school students with dyslexia. I feel like I could do more* [Online forum post]. Reddit. https://www.reddit.com/r/Dyslexia/comments/1863mr6/im_a_reading_teacher_for_middle_school_students/

Saad, R. (2017, January 4). *The arrival of dyslexia: Changes in the home*. Dyslexia Association of Singapore. https://das.org.sg/the-arrival-of-dyslexia-changes-in-the-home/

Sanctuary-Man. (2022, July 21). *Social problems linked to dyslexia?* [Online forum post]. Reddit. https://www.reddit.com/r/Dyslexia/comments/w4jrho/social_problems_linked_to_dyslexia/

Selby. (2024, February 23). *Understanding IEP goals for dyslexia: A comprehensive guide*. Everyday Speech. https://everydayspeech.com/sel-implementation/understanding-iep-goals-for-dyslexia-a-comprehensive-guide/

Shaywitz, S. (n.d.). *Signs of dyslexia*. Yale Center for Dyslexia & Creativity. https://dyslexia.yale.edu/dyslexia/signs-of-dyslexia/

Shaywitz, S. E. (2020). *Overcoming dyslexia: a new and complete science-based program for reading problems at any level*. A.A. Knopf.

Shaywitz, S. E., Holahan, J. M., Kenney, B., & Shaywitz, B. A. (2020). The Yale outcome study: Outcomes for graduates with and without dyslexia. *Journal of Pediatric Neuropsychology*, 6(4), 189–197. https://doi.org/10.1007/s40817-020-00094-3

Sheehan, M., & Wilkins, S. (2019, March 6). Targeted cognitive intervention: Changing students' learning capacity. *Carroll School*. https://www.carrollschool.org/post/~board/carroll-school-news/post/targeted-cognitive-intervention-changing-students-learning-capacity

Shichida Australia. (2023, October 15). Nurturing natural intuition in kids. *Shichida Australia*. https://www.shichida.com.au/blog/nurturing-natural-intuition-in-kids/

*16 historic figures and celebrities who have dyslexia*. (n.d.). Touch-Type Read & Spell. https://www.readandspell.com/us/famous-people-with-dyslexia

Snowling, M. J., Hulme, C., & Nation, K. (2020). Defining and understanding dyslexia: past, present and future. *Oxford Review of Education*, 46(4), 501–513. https://doi.org/10.1080/03054985.2020.1765756

Spalding, E. (2020). Children as intuitive, self-guided learners. In Erica Kleinknecht (Ed.) You don't say? Developmental science offers answers to questions about how nurture matters. *Pressbooks*. https://pressbooks.pub/hownurturematters/chapter/chapter-12/

*Spatial reasoning*. (n.d.). UK Department for Education. https://help-for-early-years-providers.education.gov.uk/mathematics/spatial-reasoning

*Success stories*. (n.d.-a). University of Michigan Dyslexia Help. https://dyslexiahelp.umich.edu/success-stories-0

*Success stories*. (n.d.-b). The Yale Center for Dyslexia & Creativity. https://dyslexia.yale.edu/success-stories/

Sutton, J. (2020, August 27). *What is intuition and why is it important? 5 examples*. Positive Psychology. https://positivepsychology.com/intuition/

TACFIT. (2014, August 28). *Scott Sonnon decoding dyslexia presentation in Michigan 2014* [Video]. YouTube. https://youtu.be/cKFQjfqJF7g?si=yq-XV0rzr6poQ8BN

*Targeted cognitive intervention*. (n.d.). Carroll School. https://www.carrollschool.org/academics/targeted-cognitive-intervention

Taylor, D. (2017, February 19). Think like there is no box. *DickTaylorBlog*. https://dicktaylorblog.com/2017/02/19/think-like-there-is-no-box/

Teachable Staff. (2023, March 15). 7 types of learning styles and how you can to teach them. *Teach:able*. https://teachable.com/blog/types-of-learning-styles

*10 famous individuals with dyslexia*. (n.d.). Parallel. https://www.parallellearning.com/post/10-famous-individuals-with-dyslexia

Theodoridou, D., Christodoulides, P., Zakopoulou, V., & Syrrou, M. (2021). Developmental dyslexia: Environment matters. *Brain Sciences*, *11*(6), 782. https://doi.org/10.3390/brainsci11060782

The Understood Team. (n.d.-a). *A day in the life of a child with dyslexia*. Understood. https://www.understood.org/en/articles/a-day-in-the-life-of-a-child-with-dyslexia

The Understood Team. (n.d.-b). *Signs of dyslexia at different ages*. Understood. https://www.understood.org/en/articles/checklist-signs-of-dyslexia-at-different-ages

[username deleted]. (2021, December 12). *What it's like to read with dyslexia* [Online forum post]. Reddit. https://www.reddit.com/r/Dyslexia/comments/rev ehl/what_its_like_to_read_with_dyslexia/

[username deleted]. (2023, August 31). *Does anyone struggle socially?* [Online forum post]. Reddit. https://www.reddit.com/r/Dyslexia/comments/166fb40/d oes_anyone_struggle_socially/

*VARK modalities: What do visual, aural, read/write & kinesthetic really mean?* (n.d.). VARK Learn Limited. https://vark-learn.com/introduction-to-vark/the-vark-mod alities/

Viktorin, J. (2021). Creativity in children and pupils with dyslexia. *Multidisciplinary Journal of School Education*, *10*(2 (20)), 15–34. https://doi.org/10.35765/mjse.20 21.1020.01

Vocabulary.com. (n.d.). Multifaceted. In *Vocabulary.com dictionary*. Retrieved July 22, 2024, from https://www.vocabulary.com/dictionary/multifaceted

Washington, J. (2023, September 7). *How dyslexic children become resilient adults?* LinkedIn. https://www.linkedin.com/pulse/how-dyslexic-children-become-resili ent-adults-jeannette-roberes/

*Was John Lennon dyslexic?* (2020, January 10). *Exceptional Individuals*. https://e xceptionalindividuals.com/about-us/blog/did-john-lennon-have-dyslexia-blog/

Watson, K. (2022, July 7). *Narrative reasoning and dyslexia*. Dyslexia in Adults. https://www.dyslexiainadults.co/post/narrative-reasoning-and-dyslexia

Weaver, P. (2023, March 13). Best quotes from famous dyslexics. *Learning Success*. https://www.learningsuccessblog.com/blog/dyslexia/best-quotes-famous -dyslexics

WeCanAllWin. (2019, March 5). *A success story, my story* [Online forum post]. Reddit. https://www.reddit.com/r/Dyslexia/comments/axjwpg/a_success_story _my_story/

Welch, M. (2023, June 2). Dyslexia and entrepreneurship: A competitive edge. *Forbes*. https://www.forbes.com/sites/forbesbusinesscouncil/2023/06/02/dysle xia-and-entrepreneurship-a-competitive-edge/

Wen, W., Zhang, X., Wu, K., Guan, L., Huang, A., Liang, Z., Yu, X., Gu, Q., & Huang, Y. (2024). Association between parenting styles and dyslexia in primary school students: the mediating role of home literacy environment. *Research Square*. https://doi.org/10.21203/rs.3.rs-3873207/v1

*We're here to empower dyslexic thinking*. (n.d.). Made by Dyslexia. https://www.m adebydyslexia.org/

*What is dyslexia?* (n.d.). British Dyslexia Association. https://www.bdadyslexia.or g.uk/dyslexia/about-dyslexia/what-is-dyslexia

*Why creativity matters – and how we can nurture it*. (n.d.). Learning through Play. https://learningthroughplay.com/explore-the-research/why-creativity-ma tters-and-how-we-can-nurture-it

Why develop logical reasoning skills in a child? (2022, June 14). *House of Soft Skills*. https://houseofsoftskills.com/blog/logical-reasoning-skills-in-a-child

Wilde, J. (2016, December 30). For Packers' Joe Whitt, overcoming dyslexia leads to growth as a coach. *ESPN Wisconsin Blog*. https://www.espn.com/blog/milwaukee/post/_/id/1061/you-grow-from-st ruggle-for-packers-joe-whitt-overcoming-dyslexia-leads-to-growth-as-a-coach

Wilkins, S. (2020, March 9). The best approach for dyslexia education: Strengths-based or remedial. *Carroll*

*School*. https://www.carrollschool.org/post/~board/head-of-school-blog/post/b est-approach-for-dyslexia-education-strengths-based-or-remedial

Wissell, S., Karimi, L., Serry, T., Furlong, L., & Hudson, J. (2022). "You don't look dyslexic": Using the job demands—resource model of burnout to explore employment experiences of Australian adults with dyslexia. *International Journal of Environmental Research and Public Health*, *19*(17), 10719. https://doi.org/10.339 0/ijerph191710719

Yazar, S., Soğancı, S., Öğrenciler, D., Üzerindeki, O., Etkileri -İlgili, P., Derlemesi, A., & Kulesza, E. (2023). Psychosocial effects of dyslexia in terms of students, parents, and school community-research review. *Turkish Journal of Special Education Research and Practice 2023*, *5*(1), 1–17. https://doi.org/10.37233/TRSPED.2023.0134

Made in the USA
Columbia, SC
27 May 2025

58539488R00117